# Information Literacy Instruction

## CHANDOS
### INFORMATION PROFESSIONAL SERIES

Series Editor: Ruth Rikowski
(e-mail: Rikowskig-r@aol.com)

Chandos' new series of books is aimed at the busy information professional. They have been specially commissioned to provide the reader with an authoritative view of current thinking. They are designed to provide easy-to-read and (most importantly) practical coverage of topics that are of interest to librarians and other information professionals. If you would like a full listing of current and forthcoming titles, please visit www.chandospublishing.com or email wp@woodheadpublishing.com or telephone +44(0) 1223 499140.

**New authors**: we are always pleased to receive ideas for new titles; if you would like to write a book for Chandos, please contact Dr Glyn Jones on email gjones@chandospublishing.com or telephone number +44(0) 1993 848726.

**Bulk orders**: some organisations buy a number of copies of our books. If you are interested in doing this, we would be pleased to discuss a discount. Please contact on email wp@woodheadpublishing.com or telephone +44(0) 1223 499140.

# Information Literacy Instruction

## Selecting an effective model

Reviewers: To save your readers time and shipping expense, please include "*distributed in the U.S. by Neal-Schuman Publishers*" following publication information in your review. Please see attached press release for additional information.

## JOHN WALSH

Oxford Cambridge New Delhi

Chandos Publishing
Hexagon House
Avenue 4
Station Lane
Witney
Oxford OX28 4BN
UK
Tel: +44 (0) 1993 848726
Email: info@chandospublishing.com
www.chandospublishing.com

Chandos Publishing is an imprint of Woodhead Publishing Limited

Woodhead Publishing Limited
80 High Street
Sawston
Cambridge CB22 3HJ
UK
Tel: +44 (0) 1223 499140
Fax: +44 (0) 1223 832819
www.woodheadpublishing.com

First published in 2011

ISBN: 978 1 84334 627 2

© J. Walsh, 2011

British Library Cataloguing-in-Publication Data.
A catalogue record for this book is available from the British Library.

All rights reserved. No part of this publication may be reproduced, stored in or introduced into a retrieval system, or transmitted, in any form, or by any means (electronic, mechanical, photocopying, recording or otherwise) without the prior written permission of the publisher. This publication may not be lent, resold, hired out or otherwise disposed of by way of trade in any form of binding or cover other than that in which it is published without the prior consent of the publisher. Any person who does any unauthorised act in relation to this publication may be liable to criminal prosecution and civil claims for damages.

The publisher makes no representation, express or implied, with regard to the accuracy of the information contained in this publication and cannot accept any legal responsibility or liability for any errors or omissions.

The material contained in this publication constitutes general guidelines only and does not represent to be advice on any particular matter. No reader or purchaser should act on the basis of material contained in this publication without first taking professional advice appropriate to their particular circumstances. All screenshots in this publication are the copyright of the website owner(s), unless indicated otherwise.

Typeset by RefineCatch Limited, Bungay, Suffolk
Printed in the UK and USA.

Dedicated to my wife, Anne – this could not have been done without her support

# Contents

| | |
|---|---|
| *List of figures* | *ix* |
| *List of tables* | *xi* |
| *Acknowledgements* | *xiii* |
| *About the author* | *xv* |

| | | |
|---|---|---|
| | **Introduction** | **1** |
| | References | 2 |
| **1** | **Methods of instruction** | **3** |
| | What is information literacy instruction? | 3 |
| | Information literacy instruction: what has it become? | 5 |
| | Teaching methods | 9 |
| | Take-home message | 50 |
| | References | 51 |
| **2** | **Objectives of instruction** | **57** |
| | The role of assessment | 57 |
| | Measuring effectiveness of instruction | 59 |
| | Take-home message | 95 |
| | References | 96 |
| **3** | **Participant populations, library environments, and learning environments** | **101** |
| | Participants | 102 |
| | Library environments | 112 |
| | Learning environments | 117 |

|   |   | Take-home message | 124 |
|---|---|---|---|
|   |   | References | 125 |
| 4 |   | **Effective ILI methods** | **127** |
|   |   | What to consider | 127 |
|   |   | Choosing based on objective | 129 |
|   |   | Choosing based on teaching method comparison | 138 |
|   |   | Choosing based on learning-environment comparison | 143 |
|   |   | Take-home message | 146 |
|   |   | References | 148 |
| 5 |   | **The future of information literacy instruction** | **153** |
|   |   | Multi-literacy instruction | 154 |
|   |   | Transliteracies | 172 |
|   |   | Other new ideas for ILI | 174 |
|   |   | Take-home message | 176 |
|   |   | References | 178 |
|   |   | **Appendix: ACRL competencies, standards, performance indicators, and outcomes** | **185** |
|   |   | Standard One | 185 |
|   |   | Standard Two | 187 |
|   |   | Standard Three | 190 |
|   |   | Standard Four | 193 |
|   |   | Standard Five | 194 |
|   |   | **Index** | **197** |

# List of figures

| | | |
|---|---|---|
| 1.1 | ILI curriculum for ENG 101 class | 12 |
| 1.2 | ILI curriculum for PSY 101 class | 13 |
| 1.3 | Evaluation form for websites | 15 |
| 1.4 | Active learning curriculum | 25 |
| 1.5 | Jigsaw method and exercise | 30 |
| 1.6 | PBL lesson development questions and learning outcomes | 35 |
| 1.7 | Modules for CAI | 38 |
| 1.8 | Jigsaw activity for LCI | 44 |
| 1.9 | Library skills worksheet | 46 |
| 2.1 | Library usage questionnaire: pretest/posttest survey | 62 |
| 2.2 | Questionnaire on information seeking behavior | 63 |
| 2.3 | Levels of cognitive learning | 74 |
| 2.4 | The information literacy process | 78 |
| 2.5 | List of standardized knowledge tests | 80 |
| 2.6 | The Library Anxiety Scale | 94 |
| 3.1 | Learning objectives of adult learners' workshops | 105 |

# List of tables

| | | |
|---|---|---|
| 1.1 | Marketing/information literacy comparison | 8 |
| 1.2 | Teaching methods | 10 |
| 1.3 | The traditional library classroom vs. the collaborative learning environment | 29 |
| 1.4 | Teacher centered vs. learner centered instruction | 42 |
| 2.1 | Pretest/posttest research design | 68 |
| 2.2 | The revised Bloom taxonomy | 72 |
| 2.3 | Cross-impact grid | 75 |
| 2.4 | Information literacy and cognitive skills | 76 |
| 2.5 | Measuring ACRL competency standards | 84 |
| 2.6 | Terms associated with the concept of affect by various authors | 87 |
| 4.1 | Selecting effective ILI method based on program objective | 137 |
| 5.1 | Evaluation criteria for internet information | 160 |
| 5.2 | Learning objectives | 164 |
| 5.3 | Cyber literacy course: competencies | 167 |
| 5.4 | MLI accuracy evaluation criteria | 168 |

# Acknowledgements

I would like to acknowledge so many. Of course my wife, who has constantly supported me throughout my education and career. I never would have written the book without her help. My son, mom and dad, and the rest of my family for inspiring me to be the best at what I do. My mother-in-law, Lavera, for her constant support and all she has done for me over the years. My fellow employees at Cochise College Libraries, especially Pat Hotchkiss, for all the experience and content they contributed to the writing of this book. I would like to thank all my instructors and contacts at the School of Information Resources and Library Science (SIRLS) at the University of Arizona. They gave me the knowledge to write this book. And finally, to all the cited authors, thank you for your contributions to the field and this book.

# About the author

**John Walsh** is a technical services/instructional librarian at the Cochise College Libraries in Douglas, Arizona. Cochise College is a small community college in a rural county of southeastern Arizona. The Libraries have a talented staff who are actively involved with the instructional program at the college. A fundamental element of the Libraries' mission is to increase information literacy throughout the College and community. The Libraries proudly serve as the center of academic information in the county and serve a growing and diverse population.

John began his higher education at Cochise College. He received an AS in Business Administration and was the Business Graduate of the year in 2003. He continued his education at the University of Arizona in Tucson, receiving a BS in Business Administration and graduating Summa Cum Laude in 2005. He received an MLS from the School of Information Resources and Library Science (SIRLS) at the University of Arizona in 2006 and is currently finishing his class work in the PhD program at SIRLS. John began his career in library science at Cochise College Libraries in 2001 and has worked through the hierarchy of the Libraries from part time circulation supervisor to a professional librarian position. He has also worked in a part time position as the corporate librarian for the Pima County Regional Wastewater Reclamation Department (PCRWRD) in Tucson, Arizona, since 2007.

He was hired by PCRWRD to create a corporate library from a large collection of internal documents. The ever growing collection is now organized on shelves and searchable through an online catalog. As a part time circulation supervisor John developed a marketing plan for the Libraries and began teaching instructional classes for the library in 2005. He developed the Libraries' first digital collections based on the historical background of southeastern Arizona and these are now available through the Arizona Memory Project.

John has published numerous articles on a variety of topics in the field of library science including patronage of literature, marketing of libraries, digital information, classification and organization of information and information literacy instruction. His research interest focuses on information literacy instruction, specifically assessing the effectiveness of the instruction. He has completed two scientific studies measuring effectiveness of instruction. His current research is a collaborative effort with Cochise College instructors in an attempt to develop a research based learning instructional model. The model embeds a librarian in the curriculum of a course and is designed to increase student learning and promote critical thinking skills.

John is also a member of the American Library Association (ALA), the Special Libraries Association (SLA) and the Arizona Library Association (AzLA).

# Introduction

In their 1989 Final Report, the ALA's Presidential Committee on Information Literacy called information literacy a 'survival skill.' This is even more true two decades later as technology has changed library participants' knowledge acquisition behavior. Participants now acquire their information from the Internet and information literacy is essential when using the Internet as a research tool. Library participants are acquiring knowledge from a medium in which anyone can write anything they want, true or false, anonymously and without consequences. This method of acquisition is threatening the epistemological protection librarians have long been providing. There is a variety of successful methods available for information literacy instruction: as Grassian and Kaplowitz claim, a 'smorgasbord groaning with an array of choices.' (Grassian and Kaplowitz, 2001). Choosing from the extensive menu can be work intensive and time consuming. There are so many factors to consider when choosing a method, topics, contact times, and delivery modes available. These elements can be blended in any number of ways, making a decision even more challenging. Then there are the tangible and intangible factors to consider: audience, purpose (what is the objective of the program), cost, time, staff, equipment, software, facilities, materials, preparation time, stakeholder impact, participants' availability (Grassian and Kaplowitz, 2009) – all of this before considering the effectiveness of the method. Being without information literacy skills can be serious and the consequences can affect quality of life. Full participation in this information rich society requires a high level of information literacy (Gross and Latham, 2007). Librarians are the leaders in the movement for an information literate society and should be effective in providing instruction that teaches these skills. There is no one proven method that is considered most effective for ILI; the existing methods are effective in different environments and situations. This book provides practical advice to librarians and others who want to select an effective information literacy instructional method for their ILI program.

# References

Association of Research and College Libraries (1989) *Presidential Committee on Information Literacy: Final Report*. Available at http://www.ala.org/ala/mgrps/divs/acrl/publications/whitepapers/presidential.cfm#importance.

Grassian, E. and Kaplowitz, J. (2001) *Information Literacy Instruction: Theory and Practice*, second edition. New York, NY: Neal-Schuman.

Gross, M. and Latham, D. (2007) Attaining information literacy: An investigation of the relationship between skill level, self-estimates of skill, and library anxiety. *Library and Information Science Research*, 29: 332–53.

Meyer, K.R., Hunt, S.K., Hopper, K.M., Thakkar, K.V., Tsoubakopoulos, V. and Van Hoose, K.J. Assessing Information Literacy Instruction in the Basic Communication Course, *Communication Teacher*, 22(1): 22–34.

# 1

# Methods of instruction

**Abstract:** This chapter provides a brief summary of what information literacy instruction (ILI) is and what it has become in most academic libraries, describing the evolution of ILI from its conception in academic library education to the marketing tool it has developed into over the years. The chapter also defines the many forms available in academic libraries today. It outlines the different modes of instruction including traditional lecture/demonstration, active learning, computer-assisted, learner-centered and self-directed.

**Key words:** information literacy instruction, instructional methods, marketing, traditional instruction (TI), active learning instruction (AL), collaborative learning, problem-based learning (PBL), computer assisted instruction (CAI), learner-centered instruction (LCI), self-directed, independent learning (SDIL).

## What is information literacy instruction?

To describe the different methods of information literacy instruction first requires a definition of what it is. This chapter does not attempt to define information literacy yet again; there is already more than enough delineation of the term. With so many definitions for information literacy, it is amazing that anyone is able to apply it to instruction. Despite Owusu-Ansah's plea for an end to the search (Owusu-Ansah, 2004) for a definition, the debate continues. Librarians have been attempting to re-clarify the definition since the ALA produced its adequate and clear demarcation of the concept in 1989. The ALA described information literacy as a participant skill set that included recognizing an information need and locating, evaluating and using the needed information effectively (American Library Association Presidential Committee on Information Literacy, 1989). This simple set of skills has been re-conceptualized and so elaborated upon that it is hardly recognizable.

There have been many efforts to clarify the ALA's definition, adding pedagogical and conceptual advancements. Christina Doyle presented specific attributes requiring certain competencies and attached them to the process of finding, evaluating, and using information (Doyle, 1992). Carol Kuhlthau believed information literacy is a learning process and incorporated the skill set into six stages of an instructional model (1993). Christine Bruce developed a relational model presenting seven different experiences a participant encounters through information literacy (Bruce, 1997). Then there are the granddaddies of all definitions, the offerings from the Association of College and Research Libraries (ACRL) and the American Association of School Librarians (AASL). These organizations created standards from the skill set, and added performance indicators and behavioral outcomes to develop an all inclusive definition. All of these definitional efforts have established the basis for what an information literate person is, though there has been limited expansion on the find–evaluate–use principles the ALA presented in their 1989 *Final Report*.

There has been enough debate on defining information literacy. Owusu-Ansah was right when proclaiming 'enough is enough' (Owusu-Ansah, 2005) when referring to the accumulated literature defining information literacy. All the above mentioned proponents have clarified what information literacy is and what skills an information literate person should possess. Efforts should now focus on how to effectively implement this knowledge into methods of instruction to promote information literacy. Literacy by nature is a continuum, changing as an individual's goals change. Grassian and Kaplowitz claimed there is no standard definition for the term: they believe that information literacy means different things to different people and can vary from situation to situation (Grassian and Kaplowitz, 2001). This is true and highlights the importance of choosing an effective method of instruction, depending on the participant and the place. The participants' ideas of being information literate are a major consideration in defining information literacy and the ideas change over time and environment. So there will be no new definition or re-conceptualization trotted out here. For the premise of this book the ALA's original simple skill set will suffice: information literacy is defined as finding, evaluating, and using information effectively; and information literacy instruction (ILI) is teaching these skills depending on who is being taught and where the instruction takes place.

## Information literacy instruction: what has it become?

Academic librarians in the United States have been using instruction to teach participants about information for more than a century. The ideas and concepts ILI is based on were developed in the late nineteenth century. Melvin Dewey changed librarianship from a vocation to a profession in that period and at about the same time wrote an article comparing the library to a school and claimed librarians were 'in the highest sense teachers' (Dewey, 1876). Though Dewey most likely made these comparisons metaphorically, the origins of library instruction in U.S. academic libraries began to appear shortly after his 1876 article.

The late nineteenth century saw an expansion of the academic library, growing from a small campus library to the large institutions and centers of academic infrastructure found on university campuses today (Hardesty, Scmitt, and Tucker, 1986). The larger facilities developed bigger, more complex collections creating a need for instruction on their use (Lorenzen, 2001). During the last decades of the century and the first half of the twentieth century many universities, including Harvard, University of Michigan, Georgetown and Oberlin, began offering courses in library and information use. During this time many academic librarians conducted research on library instruction and implemented the subject into curriculums from full semester for-credit courses to integrated single class lectures. Although pioneers of academic library instruction from this early period laid the foundations for ILI, academic library instruction did not fully develop in academic librarianship until the 1960s.

Patricia Knapp's work combining librarianship with instruction in the early 1960s started a formalized movement and brought instruction to the forefront in academic libraries. Knapp believed that library instruction should be essential to college curriculums, and her competency tests and instructional assignments continue to provide direction for today's instructional librarians (Grassian and Kaplowitz, 2001). Knapp's efforts at bibliographic instruction blossomed into the modern instructional movement that became ubiquitous in academic and school libraries in the 1980s and 1990s. Patricia Breivik redefined library instruction as information literacy while chairing the ALA Presidential

# Methods of instruction

Committee on Information Literacy which presented the find, evaluating and use definition in 1989 (Grassian and Kaplowitz, 2009). The committee did not see the concept restricted to libraries and, driven by technological progress and the explosion of information, ILI expanded. Formalized ILI programs began appearing outside of academic institutions in public and special libraries.

According to Grassian and Kaplowitz, these formalized programs forked into two branches of instruction, synchronous and asynchronous. Asynchronous is a term used to describe anytime–anyplace instruction and is delivered through workbooks or online tutorials. Synchronous is real-time face-to-face instruction, usually delivered to groups and commonly in one-shot, one-hour lectures. These one-time instructional sessions have become the most popular delivery method of ILI. 'One-shots' are a marketing tool rather than anything else. Librarians are not teaching when they are invited to perform a one-class period lecture on the use of the library and its resources; they are marketing. Susan Ardis, an experienced library instructor and Head of the Science and Engineering Libraries Division at the University of Texas Libraries, believes ILI has become strictly a practice of marketing. She claims, 'Information literacy instruction as it is typically practiced today is not truly teaching. Rather, it is a form of marketing where the action takes place in a classroom and librarians are guest lecturers demonstrating and marketing our resources, expertise, and utility. This activity is marketing' (Ardis, 2005). Presenting new resources in an orientation is like introducing new products to a target market. New student and new faculty orientations are similar to entering new market territories. Table 1.1 makes the point by comparing basic marketing goals with those of library instruction.

Librarians have their most extensive contact with students through ILI sessions and in many cases, other than reference

## Information Literacy Instruction

**Table 1.1** Marketing/information literacy comparison

| Marketing | Information literacy/bibliographic instruction |
|---|---|
| Introduce new products | Introduce new library services/tools |
| Extend or regain market for existing products | Extend usage of library tools |
| Enter new territories | Inform new students/faculty |
| Boost sales of a particular product | Increase usage of a particular tool or service |
| Cross-sell or bundle one product with another | Demonstrate how specific tools and services work together—e.g. EI and INSPEC |
| Refine a product | Improve reference services |

*Source*: Ardis (2005)

interviews, ILI is their only student contact opportunity. Ardis describes the one-shot ILI as a chance to sell the library's products to a large group of 'pre-qualified customers.' Barbara Kenney, an instructional librarian from Roger Williams University, also believes the goal of basic ILI now is marketing. She claims, 'The ultimate goal of a one-shot information literacy session is to have students actively engage with the librarians and library resources in order to provide a glimpse into the many ways the library supports student learning. In short, the librarians are building a customer base through a skillful marketing enterprise' (Kenney, 2008). Over the past fifty years library instruction has morphed from its humble beginnings as bibliographic instruction to information literacy instruction. In recent years its conceptualization has also somewhat changed; the learning paradigm is still based on critical thinking skills, but librarians are more often promoting the library and its resources in ILI sessions than trying to develop information literate students.

# Teaching methods

There is no shortage of offerings when it comes to information literacy instruction. The availability has been described as a 'smorgasbord groaning with an array of choices' (Grassian and Kaplowitz, 2001). Selecting an effective method can be difficult when faced with this surfeit, and an awareness of what is available is the first step before ordering from the extensive menu. From active learning to web-based tutorials, determining the best solution can be confusing without some knowledge of the ingredients. Instruction represents a wide range of topics and the most common areas for instruction are conducting library research and research strategies, using the catalog, using reference tools, an overview of the library and its resources, literature searching, and using computerized or electronic resources. Contact times are varied and can range from 15 minutes to full class sessions across an entire semester though the most common instructional period is the traditional one hour class period. Delivery modes also vary widely – passive, interactive, asynchronous, synchronous, face-to-face, remotely, online, and any combination of these forms. These topics, contact times and delivery modes can be blended in any number of ways to design a teaching method. However, instructional methods usually fall into one of five categories: traditional lecture, active learning, computer-assisted instruction, learner-centered instruction and self-directed independent learning (see Table 1.2).

## *Traditional instruction (TI)*

The traditional lecture–demonstration method has been widely used in every field of education, and traditional instruction has become the most popular teaching method for information literacy programs. It favors the long

**Table 1.2**  Teaching methods

| | |
|---|---|
| Traditional instruction (TI) | Instructional material is transmitted to students from teachers, and is a passive method of learning for students. (Lecture–demonstration) |
| Active learning (AL) | Students are actively engaged in their own learning, with the instructor taking on a facilitation role. (Problem-based learning) |
| Computer-assisted instruction (CAI) | A computer is used to deliver the instruction directly to the student. (Web-based tutorials) |
| Learner-centered instruction (LCI) | Focus is on the individual student's unique learning needs. (Individual term paper counseling) |
| Self-directed, independent learning (SDIL) | Learning in which the individual has primary responsibility for his or her education. (Workbooks) |

established custom of teacher-centered instruction where the instructor talks and the learners listen. It is favored by most librarians because of the popularity of the 'one-shot' single class period instructional sessions. Librarians are limited by time constraints and the lecture method seems most appropriate to deliver all the information in the short time allotted for their instruction periods. Perhaps the greatest advantage of the lecture method is control. The librarian has control over the aim, content, organization, pace, and direction of the presentation. The lecture can also facilitate any class size and is ideal for large-class communication. The fundamental problem with lecture–demonstration is that the method is not student-centered. The lecture method places students in a passive role and this has been proven to hinder student learning. It encourages one-sided communication and the instructor must make extra effort to identify student problems and student understanding of content.

Traditional instruction is developed based on numerous factors, including audience, course nature and curriculum, class assignments, class settings, availability of instructional tools, and instructor needs. Project specific information competence instruction and instructor collaboration have a great influence on traditional instruction. The librarian collaborates with instructors to target specific classes and class assignments in the development of the lecture–demonstration for each class orientation. The instructor communicates to the librarian the objectives of the class and the major assignments requiring research. The librarian designs a curriculum to inform the students on use of the library and highlights the library resources that would contribute to completion of the class assignments. The lecture–demonstration is usually delivered in a mediated classroom equipped with a computer, projector, and projection screen. The lecture method supports a simple outcome-based approach that is effective in the one-time instructional periods a librarian typically has with students. Here is a list of common learning outcomes a librarian may attempt to achieve with the one-shot traditional lecture instruction:

1. Increase knowledge of library and library resources
2. Understand contents and functions of specific databases
3. Search databases using efficient search terms
4. Evaluate websites
5. Find peer reviewed articles
6. Find books and articles in the library. (Weisskirch, 2007)

Content of a one-shot ILI session could include a presentation on what the library can do for the students, and a tour of the library's web page, highlighting the catalog and bibliographic databases. Additionally, there can be a introduction to citation

# Information Literacy Instruction

generators, resources to assist in different writing and citation styles (MLA, APA, and others), and information on the evaluation of websites. Figures 1.1 and 1.2 provide a basic ILI curriculum for an ENG 101 class and a PSY 101 class. Figure 1.3 is a form used by the California State University at Chico Libraries for evaluating web-based information.

With the advent of technology and the Internet, the lecture method is no longer confined to a synchronous, face-to-face

**Figure 1.1** ILI curriculum for ENG 101 class

**Library Orientation ENG 101**

- Intro – What can the library do for you (most valuable resource – librarian, answer questions on research and paper, courier services, Inter Library Loan, computer labs, books, DVD/VHS collection, audiobooks)

- Library Homepage
  - How to access page
  - Describe layout of page
  - Ask a Librarian link
  - Books/media request form; ILL request form

- Library Catalog
  - Functions
  - Classification/call numbers
  - Reserves
  - Holds

- Ebrary
  - 20,000 electronic books
  - Need registration in library and C# for access
  - Download reader, create bookshelf, highlights and notes column
  - Relevance graph
  - Read books online, no download/no e-mail, only prints 5 pages at a time

- Intro to Internet Research
  - Differences between library databases and websites
  - Evaluating online information using CRAAP assessment (see Figure 1.3)

Methods of instruction

- Proquest Database
    - Largest database – multidisciplinary, covers psychology, business, education and even nursing
    - Narrow search with suggested topics
    - Functions – create bibliography for work cited, e-mail, using MLA seventh edition
- Opposing Viewpoints
    - Viewpoint articles of current social issues, pro/con stance, expanded readings and stats tabs
    - Create bibliography, e-mail articles, MLA sixth edition
- Newsbank
    - National newspapers archived
    - Viewpoints between states and regions
- CQ Researcher
    - Overview of current topics in Congress
- JSTOR
    - Bibliographic database indexes over 1500 high quality journals, multidisciplinary
    - Publication delay, becoming more current
    - Search functions
- Citations
    - Citation machine
    - Word citation generator
    - Purdue OWL
    - MLA manual reserve materials at circ desk
- Most valuable resource in library? Your librarian

**Figure 1.2**  ILI curriculum for PSY 101 class

**Library Orientation PSY 101**

- Intro – What can the library do for you (most valuable resource – librarian, answer questions on research and paper, courier services, Inter Library Loan, computer labs, books, DVD/VHS collection, audiobooks)

(*Continued*)

# Information Literacy Instruction

**Figure 1.2** ILI curriculum for PSY 101 class (*cont'd*)

- Library Homepage
    - How to access page
    - Describe layout of page
    - Ask a Librarian link
    - Books/media request form; ILL request form

- Library Catalog
    - Functions
    - Classification/call numbers
    - Reserves
    - Holds

- Types of articles
    - Peer reviewed vs. non-reviewed
    - Scholarly vs. popular

- Ebrary
    - 20,000 electronic books
    - Needs registration in library and C# for access
    - Downloads reader, creates bookshelf, highlights and notes column
    - Relevance graph
    - Reads books online, no download/no e-mail, only prints 5 pages at a time

- CSA Illumina
    - Bibliographic database indexes two types of social sciences databases, PsycArticles (over 50 scholarly publications from the American Psychological Association) and PILOTS (biographic database, international index on traumatic stress syndrome)
    - Functions
        - Searching tips, phrase search, Boolean operators, truncation
        - Basic search and advanced search
        - Search tools, combine search and thesaurus
        - Creates bibliography, uses fifth edition MLA
        - E-mail articles

- Proquest Database
    - Largest database – multidisciplinary, covers psychology, business, education, and even nursing
    - Narrow search with suggested topics
    - Functions – create, bibliography for work cited, e-mail, using MLA seventh edition

- JSTOR
    - Bibliographic database indexes over 1500 high quality journals, multidisciplinary
    - Publication delay, becoming more current
- APA Citations
    - Purdue OWL, APA format and citation
    - Ask librarian for help
    - APA manual at circ desk
    - Instructor samples on reserve

**Figure 1.3** Evaluation form for websites

*Applying the CRAAP Test to Evaluating Web Sites (from the California State University at Chico)*

Title of website:
URL:

Directions: Use your judgment in allotting points for the various categories. Add up the points for the total score.

*Currency* (0 to 10 points)
If relevant, when was the information gathered?
When was it posted?
When was it last revised?
Are links functional and up to date?
Is there evidence of newly added information or links?

*Relevance/Coverage* (0 to 10 points)
What are the depth and breadth of the information presented?
Is the information unique?
Is it available elsewhere, in print or electronic format?
Could you find the same or better information in another source (for example, a general encyclopedia)?
Who is the intended audience? Is this easily determined?
Does the site provide the information you need?
Your overall assessment is important. Would you be comfortable using this source for a research paper?

*Authority* (0 to 10 points)
Who is the author/creator/sponsor?
Are author's credentials listed?
Is the author a teacher or student of the topic?
Does the author have a reputation?
Is there contact information, such as an e-mail address?
Has the author published works in traditional formats?

(*Continued*)

### Figure 1.3  Evaluation form for websites (cont'd)

Is the author affiliated with an organization?
Does this organization appear to support or sponsor the page?
What does the domain name/URL reveal about the source of the
    information, if anything? Example: .com. edu. gov. org. net

*Accuracy (0 to 10 points)*
Where does the information come from?
Are the original sources of information listed?
Can you verify any of the information in independent sources or from
    your own knowledge?
Has the information been reviewed or refereed?
Does the language or tone seem biased?
Are there spelling, grammar, or other typographical errors?

*Purpose (0 to 10 points)*
Are possible biases clearly stated?
Is advertising content vs. informational content easily distinguishable?
Are editorials clearly labeled?
Is the purpose of the page stated?
Is the purpose to: inform? teach? entertain? enlighten? sell? persuade?
Scoring:
45–50 Excellent
40–44 Good
35–39 Average
30–34 Borderline acceptable
Below 30 Unacceptable
What does the domain name/URL reveal about the source of the
    information, if anything? Example:. com. edu. gov. org. net
Total score: _____

Evaluation Criteria
*Currency: The timeliness of the web page.*
When was the information gathered?
When was it posted?
When was it last revised?
Are links functional and up to date?
Is there evidence of newly added information or links?

*Relevance/Coverage: The uniqueness of the content and its importance
    for your needs.*
What are the depth and breadth of the information presented?
Is the information unique? Is it available elsewhere, in print or electronic
    format?
Could you find the same or better information in another source? For
    example, a general encyclopedia?
Who is the intended audience? Is this easily determined?
Does the site provide the information you need?

> Your overall assessment is important. Would you be comfortable using this source for a research paper?
>
> **Authority:** *The source of the web page.*
> Who is the author/creator/sponsor?
> Are the author's credentials listed?
> Is the author a teacher or student of the topic?
> Does the author have a reputation?
> Is there contact information, such as an e-mail address?
> Has the author published works in traditional formats?
> Is the author affiliated with an organization?
> Does this organization appear to support or sponsor the page?
> What does the domain name/URL reveal about the source of the information, if anything?
> example: .com. edu. gov. org. net
>
> **Accuracy:** *The reliability, truthfulness, and correctness of the informational content.*
> Where does the information come from?
> Are the original sources of information listed?
> Can you verify any of the information in independent sources or from your own knowledge?
> Has the information been reviewed or refereed?
> Does the language or tone seem biased?
> Are there spelling, grammar, or other typographical errors?
>
> **Purpose/Objectivity:** *The presence of bias or prejudice/The reason the web site exists.*
> Are possible biases clearly stated?
> Is advertising content vs. informational content easily distinguishable?
> Are editorials clearly labeled?
> Is the purpose of the page stated?
> Is the purpose to inform? teach? entertain? enlighten? sell? persuade?
> What does the domain name/URL reveal about the source of the information, if anything?
> example: .com. edu. gov. org. net
> **(California State University of Chico)**

format. Now lectures can be recorded and delivered via a DVD or over the Internet through streaming media to students at any time. Though streaming video is a web based method of instruction and has long been considered part of computer assisted instruction (CAI), here it will be classified with traditional instruction because the content of most videos is lecture and demonstration by some type of instructor. Streaming media and delivering instruction through DVD can be more efficient and more effective than traditional face-to-face sessions. Research studies have shown that students who received video instruction recalled more information than students who received the same instructional content through the traditional face-to-face lecture method (Bennett et al., 2009). Streaming media is a web-delivered audio-video presentation that participants can view and download simultaneously on their own computers. Video instruction lets the student learn whenever they want and also allows the participant to view the instruction as many times as necessary.

Preparing video instruction is more complicated than developing a traditional face-to-face lecture to be delivered in a classroom. The process requires recording, editing, digitizing and delivery technology. Recording equipment consists of a camera, camera support, microphone, lighting, and studio. The cameras can be expensive and cost tens of thousands of dollars, but any consumer-grade camcorder or digital video camera will get the job done. A good sturdy tripod for support can be purchased at any camera store. If possible do not use the camcorder's built-in microphone: for best audio results purchase a wireless remote microphone that can be worn on the speaker's lapel. The video can be shot on location in the library, or a studio setting with fixed lighting will provide a much higher quality video. If the library does not have its own video department, it is inexpensive to rent a TV studio. There are numerous editing and digitizing softwares available, from expensive Avid Xpress to Adobe Photoshop Elements 1.0 and Jasc Paint Shop. To render the video in streaming format Microsoft Windows Media Encoder can be downloaded for free and used, and for delivery a web server to store the video is required (Cox and Pratt, 2002). In addition to the technology needed, there are other factors to consider when developing video instruction. First, keep the demonstrations short. Internet participants can exit with the click of a mouse and studies of participant behavior have shown they will do so unhesitatingly with anything they find uninteresting or difficult, so multiple short segments of three to four minutes will be more effective than a long detailed video (Crowther and Wallace, 2001). Content should be carefully scripted so the narration is brief, direct and descriptive. Colorful graphics and entertaining delivery also go a long way to keeping participants interested.

Whether choosing the face-to-face traditional lecture or video, both offer different advantages and disadvantages.

## Advantages of traditional lecture

- gives the instructor the chance to expose students to unpublished or not readily available material;
- allows the instructor to precisely determine the aims, content, organization, pace, and direction of a presentation; In contrast, more student-centered methods, e.g., discussions or laboratories, require the instructor to deal with unanticipated student ideas, questions, and comments;
- can be used to arouse interest in a subject;
- can complement and clarify text material;
- complements certain individual learning preferences. Some students depend upon the structure provided by highly teacher-centered methods;
- facilitates large-class communication.

## Disadvantages of traditional lecture

- places students in a passive rather than an active role, which hinders learning;
- encourages one-way communication; therefore, the lecturer must make a conscious effort to become aware of students'

problems and students' understanding of content without verbal feedback;
- requires a considerable amount of unguided student time outside of the classroom to enable understanding and long-term retention of content. In contrast, interactive methods (discussion, problem-solving sessions) allow the instructor to influence students when they are actively working with the material;
- requires the instructor to have or to learn effective writing and speaking skills.

(University of Wisconsin, Madison, 2006)

## Advantages of traditional lecture, streaming video

- Video streaming is available on demand – an attribute important to any self-directed instructional program.
- It can reach an unlimited number of participants at any given time.
- By providing basic information to large numbers of participants via this medium, librarians can concentrate their efforts on providing in-depth and one-on-one instruction and assistance.
- Today's students are comfortable with audiovisual formats and enthralled by the Internet.
- With well-crafted content, their interest can be engaged by streamed media projects.

## Disadvantages of traditional lecture, streaming video

- Equipment is needed, and even basic equipment costs money. You must budget for this or find willing collaborators and supporters who can provide what is needed.

- Careful analysis of instructional needs and thorough conceptualization of a possible project are necessary for a successful end product. If you are not comfortable with such conceptualization and planning, you should enlist help from someone who is.
- Updating may be necessary. When changes occur that affect the content of your video, you must revise the product or deliver out-of-date information. Careful planning can mitigate this problem, but it is important to consider when deciding what content to deliver via streaming.
- Bandwidth can be a barrier. Although products continuously improve, streaming still works best on high-speed Internet connections not often found in private homes. If you are hoping to deliver instruction to distance education students via a phone line, streaming media is not yet the optimal solution. (Cox and Pratt, 2002)

Despite the many disadvantages of the traditional lecture, it remains the most popular method of ILI in academic libraries. Librarians may not want to relinquish the control that the traditional lecture affords; however, many are facing the reality that a student-centered learning method has a greater retention level and is more effective overall at increasing students' usage of the library and advancing cognitive skills.

## Active learning instruction (AL)

*Tell me and I'll forget; show me and I may remember; involve me and I'll understand.*

*(Chinese proverb)*

Active learning has become a popular approach for ILI at academic libraries. It is much more than just a buzzword or pedagogical fad; it is a formal movement. From the earliest roots of library instruction in the United States, it was believed that the traditional lecture may not be the best way to teach students about the library (Lorenzen, 2001). Though active learning has received considerable attention recently in higher education and ILI, its use in education is not a new idea. It dates back to ancient Greece and the early teaching methods of Socrates. The Socratic Method relied on students interacting with each other and the teacher. Socrates did not lecture to his students – lecturing did not become popular until much later in history when large formal institutions of education were established (Lorenzen, 2001). In the late nineteenth and early twentieth centuries academic librarians introduced active learning as an instruction method and an alternative to lecturing, believing that lecturing was hindering the students' education about the library. The recent driving force behind the active learning movement in academic libraries, and in higher education in general, was a report released by the National Institute of Education in 1984 titled *Involvement in Learning: Realizing the Potential of American Higher Education*. The report was an attempt to improve students' participation in their own education and recommended that students take greater responsibility in their learning (Lorenzen, 2001). Since then the active learning approach to instruction has spread throughout higher education and attracted strong advocates within the academic library community. Librarians are incorporating active techniques into ILI traditional lectures, embracing the active learning approach, and developing a wide range of active learning ILI sessions.

Active learning stands in contrast to the traditional method of lecturing where the student is passive. The difference has been aptly compared using the metaphors of a glass jar being filled with liquid and a lamp being lit. The jar is filled by pouring liquid into the empty vessel similar to the traditional learning paradigm where an expert instructor transmits class content as the student sits passively absorbing the information. Active learning employs the latter metaphor where an instructor creates opportunities and engages students, guiding them to understand and encouraging them to apply the information during instruction. They help 'light the lamp' of student learning (University of Minnesota, 2008). There are four types of learning that fall into this category: active learning, cooperative learning, collaborative learning and problem-based learning (PBL). Each is distinguishable by core elements that differentiate between each method.

## Active learning

This method is defined as any type of instruction that engages students in their own learning process. The core elements of this method are student activity and engagement in the learning process (Prince, 2004). This can include anything that the student does in the classroom or is involved with to enhance learning subject content other than listening to the instructor's lecture. Students and their learning needs are the foundation for any active learning strategy. Strategies can include:

- writing exercises in which students react to lecture material;
- talking and listening exercises where the students provide feedback on what they have learned;
- reading exercises where the students summarize and create note checks to help process what they have read and help them develop the ability to focus on important information;
- reflection exercises, allowing students to pause for thought, to use their new knowledge to teach each other, or to answer questions on the day's topics – one of the simplest ways to increase retention;

- complex group exercises in which pairs of students apply course material to 'real life' situations and/or to new problems.

Here, the premise is learning by doing; it does not mean abandoning the traditional lecture altogether. However, instructors must take time to involve the students and give them time to work with the information being provided. Figure 1.4 provides a basic active learning session developed for a CIS 116 class at Cochise College Libraries. It includes a worksheet for students to record their research questions and key words to be used in their initial research queries.

## Cooperative learning

This subset of active learning covers group activities in which students are divided into groups of three or more, rather than alone or in pairs, and are assigned complex tasks, such as multiple-step exercises or a research project using multiple databases. It can be defined as a structured form of group work where students pursue common goals while being assessed individually. The core element held in common is a focus on cooperative incentives rather than competition to promote learning (Prince, 2004). As the term 'cooperative learning' suggests, students working in groups will help each other to learn. It employs the concept that many heads are better than one or two.

Cooperative groups encourage discussion of problem solving techniques and expose students to different learning styles and developing social skills. Group members share the various roles and are interdependent in achieving the group learning goal. While the academic task is of primary importance, students also learn the importance of maintaining group health and harmony, and respecting individual views (Saskatoon Public Schools, 2009). A simple group assignment

# Methods of instruction

**Figure 1.4** Active learning curriculum

---

CIS 116 Information literacy instruction: outline

Session 1: Introduction to information literacy

- Introduction to library resources
    - Library home page
    - Orientation packet – getting a library card, contacts, off-campus passwords
    - Library catalog
    - Demonstration of electronic databases

- Ebrary

- ProQuest

    - List of databases with descriptions

- Introduction to Internet research

    - Difference between library database and websites
    - Different types of search engines – examples: Google, AltaVista, Yahoo, etc.

- Selecting paper topic and approaching the research process

    - Identifying the topic

- Topic of interest

- Broad topic

- Narrowing the topic

- Create research question

- Brainstorm and concept – map topic
    - Approaching the research process

- Key concepts (search terms)

- Synonyms for search terms

- Type of information needed

- Handout: brainstorming search terms

- Evaluating Information

    - CRAAP assessment

*(Continued)*

## Figure 1.4  Active learning curriculum (*cont'd*)

- Explanation of the assessment – how the test works
- Handout: CRAAP test
- Lab time/student activity – librarian assigns pre-selected 3–4 websites or database article to students (or group of students). Students will use CRAAP test to determine whether source is valid or not. Students will discuss/present finding to class.

Due at start of Session 2: Paper topic, approach to searching, handout of search terms

Session 2: Locating resources for your paper

- Tips on search strategies on library databases
  - Types of searches
  - Difference between full-text and abstract and how to get full-text
- What is ILL
- How to ILL
  - Selecting search terms – what is a good search term, what is bad
- Broader search
- Narrow search
  - Searching phrases
  - Boolean operators
  - Truncation
- Lab time: Locating resources – students will spend rest of class locating resources for their paper. Librarian will wander around helping and be available for questions.

Due at end of Session 2: List of at least 3 resources.

Due at start of Session 3: List of all 6 resources.

Session 3: Citing resources

- Annotated bibliography
  - What is it
  - Why is it important
  - How to write one
- Citation styles – focusing on MLA style
  - Consistency is key!
  - Citation builders in the databases
  - Websites that show how to write a citation (i.e. OWL at Perdue)

# Methods of instruction

> - Lab time: Creating the annotated bibliography
> 
> Due at the end of Session 3: Annotated bibliography with all 6 sources.
> 
> CIS 116: Information literacy: Research question and search terms
> 
> Research question: _____
> _____
> _____
> _____
> _____
> 
> Major concepts/key words:
> _____
> _____
> _____
> 
> Key word chart:
> - Think of broader terms
> - Include some narrower terms
> - Find related terms
> - Think of synonyms
>
> | Keyword 1 | | Keyword 2 | | Keyword 3 |
> |---|---|---|---|---|
> | OR | | OR | | OR |
> | OR | AND | OR | AND | OR |
> | OR | | OR | | OR |
> | OR | | OR | | OR |

in an ILI session would be to ask students to acquire five resources on a given topic using the library's online catalog and bibliographic databases, and ask the students to follow the following instructions:

1. As a group, decide who will be the Recorder, Presenter, Timer, Organizer.

2. Everyone must contribute to group discussions and the wording on the poster.
3. The Organizer gathers and returns the materials needed for the lesson.
4. The Recorder draws the chart and writes the words on the chart.
5. The Timer keeps track of the time and makes sure everyone takes turns and contributes.
6. The Presenter presents the chart for the group when asked by the teacher.

There is an ever increasing need for interdependence, not just in education but in all levels of our society. Providing students with the tools to effectively work in a collaborative environment can be beneficial in many aspects of life outside of education. Cooperative learning is one way of providing students with a well defined framework from which to learn from each other (Saskatoon Public Schools, 2009).

## Collaborative learning

This subset refers to those classroom strategies that have the instructor and the students placed on an equal footing working together in, for example, designing assignments, choosing lesson content, and students presenting material to the class. The core element of collaborative learning is the emphasis on student interactions rather than on learning as a solitary activity (Prince, 2004). Students need to be willing to accept the challenge provided by collaborative-based learning. This means they must be heavily involved and expect to contribute to the learning process. They need to feel that their own experiences, interests, and judgments matter, and that they have some choice in the inquiries they design in collaboration with their teachers (Fitzpatrick, 1998).

Collaborative learning, like cooperative learning, is team oriented and students learn in a community-of-learners environment, where they act as community members. Students engage in many different class activities, interacting with each other and solving problems or completing tasks together. They think and talk about their thinking, and engage in problem solving techniques. The teacher acts as a motivator and develops ways to enhance student critical thinking. In this learning environment, students' independent and reflective thinking skills will be improved (Wang, 2006). The Learning Services Manager at the University of Auckland, Li Wang, believes collaborative learning increases students' performance levels. She claims, 'Through collaborative activities and interactions, teachers and librarians can provide learners with effective assistance that will enable them to perform at higher levels than they would otherwise' (Wang, 2006). Table 1.3 compares a traditional library classroom with a collaborative

Table 1.3 The traditional library classroom vs. the collaborative learning environment

| Role/content/ environment | Traditional library classroom | Collaborative learning environment |
|---|---|---|
| Role of student | Listener, observer, note taker, doing what librarian instructs | Problem solver, contributor, co-instructor, discussant, responsible for their own learning and instruction, co-designer of class activities |
| Role of librarian | Classroom manager, didactic teacher, authority of instruction | Knowledgeable co-learner, guide to student learning, motivator, co-designer of class activities |
| Content | Focus on library, highly instructor controlled and constructed and transmitted | Focus on information processes, focus on learning through class activities |
| Environment | Stuctured, competitive, formal knowledge transferred by librarian | Democratic, informal, knowledge created through collaboration of student and librarian |

learning environment. Notice that the librarian becomes a co-learner in this community learning environment, reversing roles with the student who becomes a contributor to the instruction of the class. One type of collaborative learning method is called the 'Jigsaw Method.' It was created in the 1970s by Eliot Aronson, an instructor at the University of Texas, to promote student learning and increase student motivation. More recently it has gained popularity in ILI at many academic libraries. Figure 1.5 contains a description of

**Figure 1.5** Jigsaw method and exercise

'The class is divided into small groups called jigsaw teams and the content material is divided into as many sections as there are team members. Each team is given one complete set of the material and individual team members are assigned their selection to study. Next, students break up into "expert" or "counterpart" groups which consist of all students who have the same section of information. In these expert groups students help each other learn the material and prepare a lesson for their original (jigsaw) teams. Once the students learn the material in the expert groups, they return to their jigsaw team to teach the material to their teammates and to learn the remainder of the content. The technique is similar to that of putting together a jigsaw puzzle; thus it is called the jigsaw approach.' (Anderson & Palmer, 1988) The jigsaw model can be effectively used in information literacy teaching. For example, it can be used in information resources evaluation. The teacher prepares citation information (for example, two online books, two online articles, and two websites) and copies of the evaluation criteria, from criterion 1 to criterion 4 (see Criteria below). In the class, all students are given the four evaluation criteria. The class is divided into jigsaw teams, with four members in each team. Each group is given a copy of citations that should lead them to full-text material online. After all jigsaw teams find the online books, articles, or websites, each student in each team is assigned one criterion group to study. Then students break up into 'expert' groups: the criterion 1 group, criterion 2 group, and so on. All students who are assigned criterion 1 will join the criterion 1 expert group, and so on for all other expert groups. In these expert groups, students help each other, learn the material, and prepare a lesson for their original (jigsaw) team. Once the students learn the material in the expert groups, they return to their jigsaw team to teach the material to their teammates and to learn the other criteria. The end result is students in all teams will learn how to evaluate books, journal articles, and Internet resources. Evaluation is a key component of information literacy. This activity fits within the realm of Australian and New Zealand Institute for

Information Literacy (ANZIIL) Standard Three: 'The information literate person critically evaluates information.' (Wang, 2006)

EVALUATION CRITERIA

Criterion 1: Authority

- What are the author's credentials — educational background, occupation, position, past writings, or years of experience?
- Is the author associated with a reputable institution or organization, and what are the basic values or goals of the organization or institution?
- Is the book or article written on a topic in the author's area of expertise?
- Has your lecturer mentioned this author?
- Have you seen the author's name cited in other sources or bibliographies?
- Does the author provide contact details, such as an e-mail or postal address, or phone number?
- Who is responsible for the information? (Know the distinction between author and webmaster.)
- If it is a website, is the URL appropriate? What institution (company, organization, government, university, and so on) or Internet provider supports this information?

Criterion 2: Currency

- When was the book or article published?
- Is the source current or out of date for your topic?
- Are the cited references (if any) up to its publication date?
- Is this a first edition of this publication or not? If it is a website, do the pages indicate revision dates?
- Is the material primary or secondary in nature?
- Is the information presented cited correctly?
- If it is a website, how up to date are the links (if any)?
- How many dead links are on the page?
- Are the links current or updated regularly?
- Is the information on the page outdated?

Criterion 3: Purpose

- What appears to be the purpose for the article or book? Does it inform, explain, or persuade?
- Is the information covered fact, opinion, or propaganda?

(*Continued*)

> **Figure 1.5** Jigsaw method and exercise (*cont'd*)

> - Does the information appear to be valid and well-researched, or is it questionable and unsupported by evidence?
> - Are the ideas and arguments advanced more or less in line with other works you have read on the same topic?
> - Is the author's point of view objective and impartial? Is the language free of emotion-arousing words and bias?
> - Who is the publisher?
>
> **Criterion 4: Audience**
>
> - What type of audience is the author addressing?
> - Is the article or book aimed at a specialized or a general audience?
> - Is the article or book aimed at a particular culture or gender?
> - Is this source too elementary, too technical, too advanced, or just right for your needs?
> - Is the article published in a popular magazine or a scholarly journal? (Wang, 2006)

the jigsaw method and an ILI practice exercise designed by Wang. In the information literacy collaborative learning community, students and librarians are all equal community members playing different roles than the traditional ILI method and creating knowledge, not transmitting it. Implementing collaborative learning techniques enables students to actively participate in the learning process, helps librarians develop an information literacy community of learners, and helps students reach their full potential developmental level (Wang, 2006).

## Problem-based learning (PBL)

Problem-based learning is an active learning technique by which learning takes place through the solving of real-world problems. It was pioneered with medical students at McMaster University whose website defines PBL as 'any learning environment where the problem drives the learning'

(Department of Chemical Engineering, 2006). Problems relevant to the subject content are introduced at the beginning of the lesson and are the motivation for learning throughout the instruction period. The approach challenges students to learn by engaging the problem and places them in an active problem solver role. There are several unique aspects that define the PBL approach:

- Learning takes place within the contexts of authentic tasks, issues, and problems that are aligned with real-world concerns.
- In a PBL course, students and the instructor become colearners, coplanners, coproducers, and coevaluators as they design, implement, and continually refine their curricula.
- The PBL approach is grounded in solid academic research on learning and on the best practices that promote it. This approach stimulates students to take responsibility for their own learning, since there are few lectures, no structured sequence of assigned readings, and so on.
- PBL is unique in that it fosters collaboration among students, stresses the development of problem solving skills within the context of professional practice, promotes effective reasoning and self-directed learning, and is aimed at increasing motivation for life-long learning. (Purser, 2010)

PBL is gaining in popularity and can even be integrated into the one-shot library instruction periods most favored by librarians and faculty (Kenney, 2008). PBL is a group activity: students are separated into groups and given a real-world current problem to analyze. PBL is a 'teaching strategy that takes everyday situations and creates learning opportunities from them' (Macklin, 2001). Students start by recording the information they already have about the problem and what additional information is needed to solve the problem. Then students develop a strategy for solving the problem. The librarian can act as a guide, showing the students the types of resources they will need, and how to use and evaluate the resources. The students collect the information and develop a worksheet of the resources they found. Each group can then present the information and review their performance (Kenney, 2008). The problem topic should be relevant to the discipline of the class receiving the instruction. Kenney developed the following problem for an ILI session she planned to give a Speech Communications class.

> You are the senior advisor to Senator Brittany Aguilera from New York City. In one hour she needs to give a two-minute presentation on the Children's Internet Protection Act (CIPA) to her constituents, but she doesn't know if she's in favor of it or against it. Your job is to find reliable, authoritative information from at least five different sources. The Senator is up for reelection and your job depends upon your getting accurate information fast.

In a presentation at the ACRL's Immersion Program, Deb Gilchrist presented a list of questions that can be used to develop a lesson plan for solving problems in a PBL instructional period. Figure 1.6 shows instructional goals developed by Kenney for solving the problem she presented to the Speech Communications class.

Advocates of the use of active learning in ILI claim it is more effective than traditional instruction at everything from encouraging library usage to increasing student retention rates. The method offers many advantages and benefits; however, there are some disadvantages to using an active learning technique.

## Figure 1.6  PBL lesson development questions and learning outcomes

What do you want the students to be able to do? (Outcomes)
What does the student need to know? (Curriculum)
What is the learning activity? (Pedagogy)
How will the students demonstrate the learning? (Assessment)
How will I know the student has done this well? (Criteria)
(Gilchrist, 2001)

(Outcomes)
- Use the library website and resources in order to find information.
- Use specific criteria to evaluate the information found.

(Curriculum)
- The library website, a government website, a general database and evaluation criteria.

(Pedagogy)
- Short introduction to the resources;
- Completion of a worksheet;
- Students working in teams using pre-determined resources;
- Teams pre-selected as being either in favor of or against CIPA;
- A de-briefing to ascertain the teams' positions and what information sources they used in order to come to their decisions.

(Assessment)
- Through their presentation and the evaluation of the resources;
- Completion of a worksheet that will be graded.

(Criteria)
- The students clearly articulate a viable answer to the problem with evidence from authoritative sources. (Kenney, 2008)

# Active learning advantages

1. may increase critical thinking skills in students;
2. enables students to show initiative;
3. involves students by stimulating them to talk more;
4. incorporates more student input and ideas;
5. easier to assess student learning;

6. better meets the needs of students with varying learning styles.

### Active learning disadvantages

1. librarian may need to become expert in many content areas;
2. may be difficult to organize active learning experiences;
3. requires more time and energy and may be stressful for librarian;
4. librarian may receive less favorable evaluations from students;
5. students may be stressed because of the necessity to adapt to new ways of learning;

There is a foundational shift occurring within higher education from teaching to learning and from inputs to learning outcomes. This shift is driving the popularity of active learning techniques, and research is supporting the claims that it is more effective and beneficial to student learning. It engages the students and transfers responsibility from the teacher to the student. Active learning offers a useful alternative to traditional instruction and many librarians are riding the active learning wave that is rolling through all levels of education.

## *Computer assisted instruction (CAI)*

Computer assisted instruction (CAI) refers to any instruction presented on a computer. Most ILI CAI is delivered through web-based tutorials. The web-based tutorial (WBT) is an attractive method for delivery of ILI and has become ubiquitous in academic libraries. WBT is an innovative approach in which CAI is transformed by Internet technologies. It allows participants to engage in self-directed, self-paced learning in almost any topic. Tutorials should not be a collection of information pages full of text and descriptions. Instead, they should be an interactive tool with different activities that engage the student in active learning with feedback and quizzes. A tutorial usually includes numerous modules with a variety of subjects to walk the student into becoming information literate. The subjects can include:

| | |
|---|---|
| Information literacy | Library services |
| Searching in information sources | Evaluation of Internet information |
| Location of books or articles | Plagiarism and copyright |
| Databases | Library services and resources |
| Thematic resources | |
| Search strategies | Citation |
| Catalog searching | Browsers |
| Academic journals | Plagiarism and citation |
| Internet | |

Figure 1.7 is a list of subject modules developed by the librarians at the State University of New York at Oswego.

To be effective these tutorials should be learning modules that promote the institutional needs of the library and relate the information library skills the library wishes its participants to achieve (Tobin and Kesselman, 1999). There are two important points to keep in mind when creating a web-based tutorial. First, find out exactly what it is your audience needs to learn and teach them that. Next, keep it simple and basic. When discussing the principles of designing web-based instruction the textbook *Information Literacy Instruction*

# Information Literacy Instruction

**Figure 1.7** Modules for CAI

### Module 1: Introduction to information
- Recognizing what information is
- Different ways information is organized
- (Competency 1)

### Module 2: Formulating a research question
- Brainstorming topics
- Narrowing a topic
- Creating a timeline for research
- (Competencies 1, 2)

### Module 3: Developing effective search strategies
Where to look for information:
- Print, non-print, CD-ROM, electronic library catalogs, Internet

How to look for information:
- Controlled vocabulary
- Key word searching
- Boolean searching
- Truncation
- Limiting
- Wildcards
- (Competency 2)

### Module 4: Basic information resources in various formats (print, non-print, CD-ROM, electronic library catalogs, Internet)
- Library tour
- Classification scheme (Library of Congress, Dewey, etc.)
- Background information
- Encyclopedias
- Browsing shelves
- Biographical information
- Consulting experts
- Maps
- Statistics
- (Competency 2)

# Methods of instruction

> **Module 5: Electronic library catalogs (online public access catalogs)**
> - How to search the home library's catalog effectively by author, title, subject, key word, etc.
> - How to locate the information found (i.e.: locate a book on the shelf by call number, access an online database or document, etc.)
> - (Competencies 2, 3)
>
> **Module 6: Indexes and abstracts: How they work**
> - Using information access tools in print, non-print, CD-ROM, Internet
> - Tips and techniques
> - Truncation, limiting, Boolean searching, etc.
> - (Competencies 2, 3)
>
> **Module 7: Searching the World Wide Web effectively for information**
> - (Competency 3)
>
> **Module 8: Evaluating the information you find**
> - Selecting the 'best' information by determining credibility, authority, timeliness, accuracy in a variety of formats (print, non-print, CD-ROM, Internet)
> - (Competency 4)
>
> **Module 9: Recording your information**
> - Understanding plagiarism
> - Citing information
> - Citing information in appropriate format (APA, MLA, Chicago, etc.)
> - (Competency 8)

*Source*: Staines (1998)

(2001) refers to this quote by library web designer Mark Stover: 'If content is clearly king, then need is surely emperor' (Stover and Zink, 1996). Grassian and Kaplowitz state, 'Simply designed web based materials may take great time and effort to create, yet they can make an enormous difference in insuring that significant learning takes place' (Grassian and Kaplowitz, 2001). Grassian and Kaplowitz assert the basic steps in planning instruction are always the same:

1. RECOGNIZE the participant need
2. DESCRIBE AND ANALYZE the present institutional situation and available resources
3. DEVELOP instructional goals and objectives
4. DESIGN appropriate method and materials
5. DELIVER the instruction
6. EVALUATE AND REVISE (Grassian and Kaplowitz, 2001)

Any web editing software can be used to create the tutorials, though many libraries use animation created with Flash software, video, and other graphics which can present many interactivity possibilities and add interesting visuals to the tutorials.

The spread and popularity of distance education has driven librarians to embrace CAI. While many librarians are excited about the great potential and advantages of using this medium, there are disadvantages and warnings against using CAI just for the sake of using a new technology. CAI has a number of advantages; first and foremost, it can save time that is being devoted to repetitive instruction by delivering asynchronous instruction available anytime, anywhere to participants for first time use or a review (Kaplowitz and Grassian, 2009). Another important valued benefit is that it actively involves the student in the learning process. It is impossible for the student to be a totally passive member of the situation, and this very activity and involvement facilitate learning (Chambers and Sprecher, 1980). It also allows the students to learn at their own pace. Furthermore, CAI provides immediate and systematic feedback that supports more effective student learning. The main drawback to using CAI is the fact that not all students have access to the Internet and knowledge of Internet technologies to use the tutorials.

Though this is becoming less of a problem there still remains a digital divide in participant access and knowledge.

Recent research has shown that CAI in academic libraries is still at an early stage of development and though most tutorials follow sound pedagogical strategies for instruction, there is much room for improvement (Somoza-Fernández and Abadal, 2009). Areas most in need of improvement include defining learning objective and outcomes more clearly and giving more attention to the concepts behind the mechanics of CAI. Other suggestions include increasing interactivity: 'The exercises should incorporate more elements of feedback because the existing ones are too simple. More game-type exercises should be included to complement the questionnaire-type exercise' (Somoza-Fernández and Abadal, 2009). The tutorials should also offer different levels of difficulty, such as a basic and an advanced level. Finally, CAI should develop more instructional methods to accommodate distance-learning students, and the tutorials should develop elements that enhance usability and accessibility to allow greater interactivity of the students with the system (Somoza-Fernández and Abadal, 2009). CAI is the future of ILI and will someday overtake traditional instruction as the favored method of delivery by all academic libraries. Librarians are still just learning how to achieve the full benefits of this learning tool.

## *Learner-centered instruction (LCI)*

In learner-centered instruction (LCI), learners are partners in their own learning and they learn from one another as well as from the instructor. Student involvement is the foundational element of LCI and as in active learning the student is encouraged to participate in the learning process. However, in LCI the students are not just active participants in learning, they are also active participants in instructing and teaching.

Grassian and Kaplowitz claim that the LCI approach rests on three principles, collaboration, participation and responsibility (Grassian and Kaplowitz, 2009). There is sharp contrast between LCI and teacher-centered instruction. Teacher-centered instruction is considered the banking approach to teaching by which the teacher deposits the information into the empty account of the student, metaphorically giving the student a fish. LCI teaches the student to fish and the students take on a larger role in the learning process, actually teaching themselves as they learn. Table 1.4 presents the differences between a teacher-centered classroom and a learner-centered environment. It defines the principles mentioned by Grassian and Kaplowitz, as students collaborate with other students

**Table 1.4** Teacher-centered vs. learner-centered instruction

| Teacher-centered | Learner-centered |
| --- | --- |
| Focus is on instructor | Focus is on both students and instructor |
| Focus is on language forms and structures (what the instructor knows about the language) | Focus is on language use in typical situations (how students will use the language) |
| Instructor talks; students listen | Instructor models; students interact with instructor and one another |
| Students work alone | Students work in pairs, in groups, or alone, depending on the purpose of the activity |
| Instructor monitors and corrects every student utterance | Students talk without constant instructor monitoring; instructor provides feedback/correction when questions arise |
| Instructor answers students' questions about language | Students answer each other's questions, using instructor as an information resource |
| Instructor chooses topics | Students have some choice of topics |
| Instructor evaluates student learning | Students evaluate their own learning; instructor also evaluates |
| Classroom is quiet | Classroom is often noisy and busy |

Source: http://www.nclrc.org/essentials/goalsmethods/learncentpop.html

and the instructor by taking on more instructional and learning responsibility through their participation. The center of power and authority of the teacher-centered classroom is diffused, with students seeking out knowledge rather than knowledge primarily coming from the teacher.

The idea behind LCI is to empower students in the learning process and cultivate life-long learning skills. Instead of instruction being delivered in the form of information-laden lectures, lessons are designed to engage students in learning experiences that enable them to learn content and 'learn how to learn' at the same time (Cuseo, 2006). The students are not passive learners, sitting in a classroom listening to the instructor. They are engaged learners participating as active agents in the learning process. The instructor's role also changes from a 'knowledge-laden professor' to a class facilitator, coaching the students while they instruct themselves. The 'sage on the stage' becomes the 'guide by the side' (Cuseo, 2006).

One of the major limitations attached to library instruction is the problem of connectedness. The students are confronted with a new teacher and with content that they realize will not be graded or assessed. Consequently the students do not feel connected to the instructor or the material and they do not talk or engage with each other. An LCI approach is a possible solution to this connectedness problem. Michael Lorenzen, an academic librarian at Central Michigan University, designed an LCI lesson plan for use in a 90-minute library instructional period. He claims this technique was successful at overcoming the connectedness limitation. He used an LCI technique called a jigsaw. In a jigsaw activity, instructional content is broken into several small parts and the class is divided into several small groups. Each part is assigned to a group; the groups analyze the material, working among themselves to develop a presentation about the material. The groups then reform as a class and present what they have learned about their part. As the groups are teaching the class about their content, the instructor acts as a facilitator, adding expertise to the process and filling in any relevant points the groups may have missed. Figure 1.8 has a description of the lesson plan Lorenzen used.

### Figure 1.8  Jigsaw activity for LCI

This activity requires a mediated computer lab where the instructor has access to a computer connected to a projector and a projection screen. Each student has access to a computer. Before the assignment is handed out, the librarian begins class by lecturing on several topics including the importance of limiting a search topic and how to use the online catalog. After this introduction, the jigsaw activity is explained. The jigsaw assignment requires students to think about separate bibliographic databases available on the library website. Examples include Opposing Viewpoints ProQuest, Lexis-Nexis, and JStor. The class is divided into groups consisting of 4 to 5 students each. These groups are then asked to learn about one of the databases.

The students are provided with a list of questions to answer about the databases.

1. What is the scope of this database? What is included? Why would you use it?
2. How do you start a search? Is there more than one collection to choose from at the initial screen?
3. What are some of the options for advanced searching?
4. How do you e-mail or print off results?
5. What did you like about this database?
6. What did you dislike about this database?

Inform the students before beginning that they will be asked to share what they learned with the entire class. Each group selects one spokesperson who will speak about the group findings.

Each group is given 25 minutes to find the information about the database. Each group has access to computers for each group member. During this time, the librarian walks around and helps each group. After the 25 minutes passed, each group talks for about 5 minutes about the database. The presenter is allowed to use the instructor PC in the classroom that was projecting on a screen. The librarian added details as each student spoke and corrected any erroneous details.

The librarian concludes the class with an overview of what has been covered during the lesson, covering points about the databases the students may have missed and the students are given an opportunity to ask any additional questions.

*Source*: Lorenzen (2004)

LCI has many advantages. For example, students obtain information and direction from themselves and do not rely on gaining these from the teacher. It helps the student develop leadership skills and become familiar with the role of information provider instead of passive learner. Additional benefits to both student and teacher are that students learn to problem solve by themselves, and the teacher is exposed to new learning experiences and lessons. There are also disadvantages. For example, the open-ended lesson plans of LCI may not give enough direction for students to obtain the intended knowledge and skills. Also, students often need encouragement to stay on task and may lack the initiative and motivation to get all the required work done to disseminate the information to the whole class. Finally, students need teachers to be more than a facilitator; the teacher has to command accountability so that students learn to listen to the teacher when necessary. LCI requires a balance between teacher-centered and participant-centered instruction and an effective LCI lesson plan incorporates elements of both (ELED Blog, 2006).

## Self-directed, independent learning (SDIL)

In SDIL students take the primary responsibility for their own education. They take the initiative of what occurs, and select, manage, and assess their own learning activities. The activities can be pursued at any time, in any place, by any means, asynchronously or synchronously. The activities can be delivered through handouts, workbooks, both physical hard copies and web-based tutorials. A basic library skills worksheet is depicted in Figure 1.9. Materials and content are provided to the students and they complete the lessons at their own pace. Self-directed learning requires a commitment

### Figure 1.9   Library skills worksheet

### Library skills worksheet from Cazenovia College 2009

Finding a book we have in the library:

> Go to The TOWER
>
> Using the navigation arrow select searching by Author
>
> Search by Author (Remember when searching for author, type in last name first)
>
> Type in Hemingway, Ernest
>
> How many entries are there on the author Ernest Hemingway_____?
>
> Scroll down to entry six and double click on the title of the book.
>
> Write down the call number_____.
>
> Where is the location of the book in the library_____?
>
> What is the status of the book_____?

Limiting your search on The TOWER to material type:

Example: videos

At the main screen:

> Select Advanced Searching
>
> Type in the words **children** in the first 'Any Field' search box
>
> Then find 'Limit' by material type
>
> Click on navigation arrow and select 'video'
>
> Point and click on 'Submit'
>
> How many videos do you find on the subject_____?

Using Microfilm:

Go to the microfilm room and locate the collection of the *New York Times*. Choose the one that includes your birth date. Make a copy of the first page (attach the copy to the worksheet).

***Microfilm copies cost 5-cents; change can be made at the circulation desk.

Finding a Journal Article:

Using the library's research computers, examine the library web page (it should default to that address). Click onto **Research Database** and select one of them; locate an article dealing with a subject related to your major.

Please answer the following questions concerning the selected article:

> Database selected: _____

# Methods of instruction

Title of article: _____
Source, i.e. the name of the journal, magazine or newspaper:
_____

Date of the article _____
Author or byline _____
Web address of the database _____

**Requesting an article through Interlibrary Loan:**

Using one of the research databases, search for an article using the keywords **violence in schools**. Pick one that is not available in full text or in the library's collection. Fill-out an interlibrary form below:

INTERLIBRARY LOAN –REQUEST FOR ARTICLES

Fill out completely, with NO ABBREVIATIONS

Incomplete/illegible forms will not be processed

RETURN THIS FORM TO THE REFERENCE LIBRARIAN

Today's date:__/__/___
Your name:_____ Your box#_____
Title of Magazine/Journal: _____
ISSN:_____-_____(will be an eight digit number)
On computer printouts, it will be near the journal title
Volume #:____ Issue #:_____ Pages:_____
Complete date of aticle: _____
Author(s): _____
Title of aticle: _____

**Meet the Librarian:**

1. Go to the Reference Module Kiosk or the Reference Office behind it.
2. Say 'hello' and have the Reference Librarian autograph your workbook
3. If you have any concerns or problems using the library, ask the librarian for help. We are here to answer any questions.

**Equine Area:**

Using the TOWER search for the subject **horse** and follow the directions for limiting your search to journal. Find how many equine magazines the college subscribes to. Name three of them:

1. _____
2. _____
3. _____

(*Continued*)

Information Literacy Instruction

**Figure 1.9** Library skills worksheet (cont'd)

Juvenile Literature:

Using The TOWER, search under title. Type: **In the Night Kitchen** and answer the following questions:

1. Who is the author? _____
2. Are there illustrations? _____
3. What is the location of the book? _____
4. On what floor is the **Juvenile** section located in the library?
   _____
5. By looking at the bibliographic record for this title, explain what the book is about _____

\*\*\*If you find yourself having trouble please ask a librarian for assistance.

Using the Limiting Capabilities of 'The Tower'

1. In the 'Any Field' box type in a subject that your find interesting.
2. Limit the search to year of publication.
3. Type in After 1993 and Before 2003.
4. Point and click on submit.
5. Give the title of one of the books published after 1993. _____
   _____
   _____

Another exercise for using the Limit Your Search feature of the TOWER:

Search for a bible that the library has in its collection that was published before the year 1600. NOTE: Search by subject and follow above directions for limiting your search. Please answer the following questions:

1. What year was this book published? _____
2. What language was the book written in? _____
3. What is the location of the book? _____
4. Where in the library would you actually have a chance to see this item on display? Circle the correct answer:

   A. Main floor              C. Cazenoviana Room
   B. Basement level          D. Circulation desk

Try limiting your search in other ways to see what results you can obtain. The advanced search option lets you limit by location, language, year, publisher, and material type. The TOWER contains a wealth of information and will be a great asset when locating material in the library.

*Source*: Casenovia College (2009) http://www.cazenovia.edu/default.aspx?tabid=705

from the student. Grassian and Kaplowitz claim that being a self-directed learner is a characteristic of the learner, not the methodology or instruction (Grassian and Kaplowitz, 2009). The self-directed learner goes beyond the material presented in the worksheets, exploring other resources to expand on the learning experience, and looks for supplemental material to help them understand the lessons.

Supporters of SDIL claim it is the most effective method for actively engaging the student in the learning process. They believe SDIL personalizes the learning experience and motivates the students to discover things by themselves. There are many advantages and disadvantages when using the self-directed method.

## Advantages of SDIL

- supports active engagement of the learner in the learning process;
- fosters curiosity;
- enables the development of life-long learning;
- personalizes learning experience;
- highly motivating as it allows learners the opportunity to experiment and learn by themselves;
- builds on learners' prior knowledge;
- creates a joy of learning;
- enables students to learn at their own pace.

## Disadvantages of SDIL

- requires strong commitment from learner;
- many not used to being self-directed learners;
- lack of feedback from instructor;

- lesson content may not contain information needed by learner to understand subject;
- requires complex initial framework and structure.

The popularity and convenience of web-based instruction demand that librarians develop new ways for students to learn independently. Though face-to-face one-shots are still the standard for ILI, the future is web-based instruction and students will insist that the instruction be available asynchronously so that they can take advantage of it whenever and wherever they want.

## Take-home message

This chapter described what ILI is and what it has become. Though the concept has evolved over the years from teaching students to be information literate to an outreach marketing approach, librarians still have the original goal driving their ambitions, to teach participants how to find, evaluate and use information effectively. The chapter also introduced the various methods of instruction that are available. The traditional method continues to be the most popular with academic librarians because of its convenience and the time constraints involved in prioritizing instructional time within class periods. Active learning methods have been used in web-based tutorials from the beginning, and academic librarians are also experimenting with the active learning methods in face-to-face sessions. This will gain popularity as the shift in learning paradigms spreads throughout higher education. Many traditional lecture sessions already employ more than one method in their delivery. The future of ILI is in computer-assisted instruction and as distance learning is used in a greater percentage of the classes offered, CAI will become

Methods of instruction

the standard. Knowing what methods are available is just the first step when deciding on which method would best work for your institution and situation. There are many other elements in the equation for selecting an effective method, and the next chapter presents one of the most significant. Defining the objectives of your ILI program will most likely narrow your choice and answer many questions in determining which method will be most effective for your participants.

# References

American Library Association Presidential Committee on Information Literacy. (1989) *Final Report.* American Library Association, Chicago, IL.

Anderson, F. and Palmer, J. (1988) The Jigsaw Approach: Students Motivating Students. *Education 109*, no. 1(59).

Ardis, S. (2005) Instruction: Teaching or Marketing? *Issues in Science and Technology Librarianship.* Available at *http://www.istl.org/05-spring/viewpoints.html.*

Bennett, B., Dacio, H., Logan, T., Rousseau-Smith, M. and Strathman K. (2009) Video Instruction Versus Traditional Lecture: Recalling Simple Steps. Master Thesis, Califorinna State University, San Bernardino available *at http://emurillo .org/Classes/Class2/documents/VideoInstruction.doc.*

Bruce, C.S. (1997) *Seven Faces of Information Literacy.* Adelaide: Auslib Press.

Campbell, S. (2004) Defining Information Literacy in the 21st Century. Paper presented at the World Library and Information Congress: 70th IFLA General Conference and Council, August 22–27, Buenos Aires, available at: *www.ifla.org/IV/ifla70/papers/059e-Campbell.pdf.*

Casenovia College. (2009) Library Skills Worksheet. Available at *http://www.cazenovia.edu/default.aspx?tabid=705.*

Chambers, J. and Sprecher, J. (1980) Computer Assisted Instruction: Current Trends and Critical Issues. Available at *http://www.csuvc.com/drupal/files/ed1.pdf*.

Crowther, K. and Wallace, A. (2001) Delivering Video-Streamed Library Orientation on the Web. *College & Research Libraries News*, 62(3): 280–5.

Cox, C. and Pratt, S. (2002) The Case of the Missing Students and How We Reached Them Through Streaming Video. *Computers in Libraries,* 22(3): 40–5.

Cuseo, J. (2006) The Case for Learner-Centered Education. On Course Workshop, Student Success Strategies. Available at *http://www.oncourseworkshop.com/Miscellaneous018.htm*.

Department of Chemical Engineering. (2006) Problem-based learning especially in the context of large classes. Available at *www.chemeng.mcmaster.ca/pbl/pbl.htm*.

Dewey, M. (1876). The Profession. *American Library Journal*, 1 (September), pp. 5–6.

Doyle, C. (1992) *Outcome Measures for Information Literacy within the National Education Goals of 1990: Final Report of the National Forum on Information Literacy. Summary of Findings*. Washington, DC: US Department of Education. (ERIC document no; ED 351033). Available at *http://eric.ed.gov/ERICDocs/data/ericdocs2/content_storage_01/0000000b/80/23/4a/12.pdf*.

ELED 3110 Blog. (2006) Available at *http://eled3110asturgill.blogspot.com/2006/08/most-of-us-are-very-familiar-with.html*.

Fitzpatrick, C. (1998) Information Literacy and Learning. Available at *http://www.edu.pe.ca/bil/bil.asp?ch1.s4.gdtx*.

Fosmire, M. and Macklin, A. (2002) Riding the Active Learning Wave: Problem-Based Learning as a Catalyst for Creating Faculty–Librarian Instructional Partnerships. Available at *http://www.istl.org/02-spring/article2.html*.

Gilchrist, D. (2001) *Institute for Information Literacy Immersion Program*.

Grassian, E. and Kaplowitz, J. (2001) *Information Literacy Instruction: Theory and Practice*, second edition. New York, NY: Neal-Schuman.

Grassian, E. and Kaplowitz, J. (2009) *Information Literacy Instruction: Theory and Practice*, third edition. New York, NY: Neal-Schuman.

Hardesty, L.L., Scmitt, J.P. and Tucker, J.M. (1986). *Participant Instruction in Academic Libraries: A Century of Selected Readings*. Metuchen, NJ: Scarecrow Press.

Kenney, B. (2008) Revitalizing the One-Shot Instruction Session Using Problem-Based Learning. Available at *http://docs.rwu.edu/cgi/viewcontent.cgi?article=1012&context=librarypub*.

Koufogiannakis, D. (2006) Effective methods for teaching information literacy skills to undergraduate students: A systematic review and meta analysis. Accessed 5 September 2009 at *http://ejournals.library.ualberta.ca/index.php/EBLIP/article/viewArticle/76*.

Kuhlthau, C.C. (1993) *Seeking Meaning: A Process Approach to Library and Information Services*, Norwood, NJ: Ablex Publishing Corporation.

Lorenzen, M. (2001) *Brief History of Library Instruction in the United States of America*. Illinois Libraries. Available at *http://www.libraryinstruction.com/lihistory.html*.

Lorenzen, M. (2001) Active Learning and Library Instruction. Available at *http://www.libraryinstruction.com/active.html*.

Lorenzen, M. (2004) Encouraging Community in Library Instruction: A Jigsaw Experiment in a University Library Skills Classroom. Available at *http://www.libraryinstruction.com/jigsaw.html*.

Macklin. A. (2001) Integrating Information Literacy Using Problem-Based Learning. *Reference Services Review*, 29(4): 307.

National Institute of Education. (1984) Involvement in Learning: Realizing the Potential of American Higher Education. Available at *http://www.eric.ed.gov/ERICDocs/ data/ericdocs2sql/content_storage_01/0000019b/80 /32/05/78.pdf.*

Owusu-Ansah, E.K. (2003) Information Literacy and the Academic Library: A Critical Look at a Concept and the Controversies Surrounding It. *Journal of Academic Librarianship*, 29: 219–30.

Owusu-Ansah, E.K. (2005) Debating Definitions of Information Literacy: Enough is Enough. *Library Review*, 54(6): 366–74.

Prince, M. (2004) Does Active Learning Work? A Review of Research. Available at *http://www4.ncsu.edu/unity/ lockers/participants/f/felder/public/Papers/Prince_AL.pdf.*

Purser, R. (2010) Center for Creative Inquiry, Teaching Philosophy. Available at *http://online.sfsu.edu/~rpurser/ revised/pages/problem.htm.*

Saskatoon Public Schools. (2009) Instructional Strategies Online. Available at *http://olc.spsd.sk.ca/de/pd/instr/ strats/coop/index.html.*

Somoza-Fernández, M. and Abadal, E. (2009) Analysis of Web Based Tutorials Created by Academic Libraries. *The Journal of Academic Librarianship*, 35(2): 126–31.

Staines, G. (1998) Web-Based Course Task Force. The SUNY Council of Library Directors, Final Report. Available at *http://www.sunyconnect.suny.edu/ili/scld.htm.*

Stover, M. and Zink, S.D. (1996) World Wide Web Home Page Design: Patterns and Anomalies of Higher Education Library Home Pages. *Reference Service Review*, 24(3): 7–20.

Teacher vs. Learner-Centered Instruction. Available at *http://www.nclrc.org/essentials/goalsmethods/learncentpop.html*.

Tobin, T. and Kesselman, M. (1999) Evaluation of Web-Based Library Instructional Programs. Available at *http://archive.ifla.org/IV/ifla65/papers/102-163e.htm*.

University of Minnesota. (2008) What is Active Learning? Center for Teaching and Learning. Available at *http://www1.umn.edu/ohr/teachlearn/tutorials/active/what/index.html*.

University of Wisconsin, Madison, Center for the Integration of Research, Teaching and Learning. (2006) Advantages and Disadvantages of the Traditional Lecture Method. Available at *http://cirtl.wceruw.org/diversityresources/resources/resource-book/advantagesanddisadvantagesofthetraditionallecturemethod.htm*.

Wang, L. (2006) Sociocutural Lear'ning Theories and Information Literacy Teaching Activities in Higher Education. Available at *http://vnweb.hwwilsonweb.com/hww/results/external_link_maincontentframe.jhtml;hwwilsonid=DHWR3NYRPSAUFQA3DIKSFGGADUNGIIV0*.

Weisskirch, R.S. and Silveria, J.B. (2007) The Effectiveness of Project Specific Information Competence Instruction. *Research Strategies*, 20: 370–8.

# 2

# Objectives of instruction

**Abstract:** This chapter identifies the measures of success when determining the effectiveness of ILI. Cognitive outcomes, measuring changes in knowledge, are considered a standard by many ILI programs; however, these are only one aspect of determining effectiveness. This chapter describes different cognitive outcomes as well as behavioral outcomes which measure changes in actions, and affective outcomes that measure changes in attitudes and values. The behavioral outcomes address increases in student library usage and information seeking behavior of participants. The cognitive outcomes include increased learning skills and library skills. The affective outcomes involve decreasing library anxiety and increasing student self-efficacy.

**Key words:** information literacy instruction effectiveness, information literacy instruction assessment, cognitive learning outcomes, behavioral learning outcomes, affective learning outcomes, self-efficacy, library anxiety.

# The role of assessment

In the twenty-first century, assessment has become an integral part of higher education and one of the driving forces behind this movement is accountability (Radcliff et al., 2007). In the 1970s, several changes in higher education brought about the cry for accountability. Many universities faced a financial crisis, the population of students attending college became more diverse, and concerns were raised that college graduates did not have the skills and abilities needed in the workplace. The value of higher education came to be questioned by the public and politicians (Northern Illinois University, 2010). Four reports were issued in the 1980s, *The Access to Quality Undergraduate Education, Integrity in the College Curriculum, Involvement in Learning*, and *To Reclaim a Legacy*, that brought accountability to the forefront in higher education. The results of these reports produced specialized accreditation bodies and a demand for an outcomes approach to evaluation in higher education instruction. What began as an external influence on education has grown into an internal force: improvement as accountability (Northern Illinois University, 2010).

As the accountability movement progressed, information literacy became a general educational requirement at public institutions in higher education. The six regional accreditation organizations of higher education and several professional and disciplinary accrediting organizations have included information literacy in their standards, either implicitly or explicitly (Saunders, 2007). The academic library has always been the leader in promoting information literacy within higher education, and the decision to make it an educational requirement obligated academic libraries to address how they would measure success within their instructional programs. The Association of College and Research Libraries (ACRL) have developed a set of competency standards for information literacy in higher education (see Appendix) to evaluate the information literate student. Many libraries that use cognitive outcomes to determine effectiveness use the standards to measure the success of their programs. Connecting success with learning outcomes was a logical choice for academic libraries because it associated the library with institutional instructional goals and attached the library to the instructional process. Many libraries use cognitive outcomes to determine effectiveness, and with the evolution of ILI to become a marketing tool the measures of other options were explored to determine instructional effectiveness. Other measures of effectiveness use the measures defined by the specialized accreditation organizations that evaluate the academic standards. For example, the *Handbook for Accreditation of the North Central Association of Colleges and Schools* (NCA) includes a criterion that demands organizations learning resources from the library support student learning and that it is critical for colleges to assess actual student use of the resources (NCA, 2003). Using these measures, a library could determine effectiveness by measuring students' increased usage of the library after receiving library instruction. Whatever measure an academic library chooses to use, institutional assessment has to be considered before any decision is made.

## Measuring effectiveness of instruction

When selecting an effective method of ILI for a specific situation, first one must define what will determine the success of the ILI program. A program needs to determine what the instructional goals will be to assess the effectiveness of teaching methods. When developing an ILI program, assessment of effectiveness should be one of the earliest considerations and should be 'built into the planning process from the very beginning' (Grassian and Kaplowitz, 2009). There are many aspects that determine success and most can be classified into three categories: changes in cognitive outcomes, changes in behavioral outcomes and changes in affective outcomes. Changes in cognitive outcomes can be as small as remembering facts to applying what was taught to a new situation and may require more than a simple survey to collect results. Behavioral changes most often involve students increasing their usage of the library and participant information seeking behaviors. The changes can usually be measured through self-administered surveys. Affective changes including decreases in library anxiety require long survey questionnaires and a comparison of test results against a Library Anxiety Scale (LAS). Choosing the instructional goal is a major factor in the equation for selecting an effective method for a particular environment.

## *Behavioral outcomes*

Behavioral outcomes are changes in action (e.g., improved and increased use of online library resources; improved and increased use of librarians; improved and increased use of the physical library itself). ILI programs are the most common outreach used by academic libraries today, and most often the outreach instructional goals are to get the student to use the library and its resources. Library usage is essential to the academic library maintaining a physical presence on college campuses and should be considered a primary objective in promoting the library and its resources. The Cochise College Library director, Pat Hotchkiss, believes the primary objective of most ILI is to promote use of the library and its resources. She claims, 'It's all about getting the students to start using our databases and coming in the door.' Student usage also drives the expenditures on resources (Hotchkiss, 2007, 2009). Academic libraries allocate their budget using a formula of student usage, educational priorities, and materials cost (Trombley, 2003). 'Facing yearly budgetary constraints, accountability has become essential to academic libraries' success in today's competitive environment' (Trombley, 2003). Any consistent decrease in student usage will result in a reduction of the library budget. Comparatively, increased student usage statistics are sufficient justification for additional funds (Trombley, 2003; Hotchkiss, 2007). In the late 1990s two prominent researchers performed a longitudinal study to explain the use of library facilities at that time. The study, published in a 2001 issue of *Library Trends*, showed 'one's familiarity with the library had the greatest impact on library use' (Simmonds, 2001: 630). Instruction has become the most popular method to advance student familiarity with library resources.

Library usage is a fundamental variable in determining many aspects of an academic library: it regulates hours of operation, budgetary decisions are based on increases and decreases of usage, and it controls resource acquisition and weeding. The importance of student usage to the infrastructure of the academic library makes usage an appropriate and important measurement of effective instruction. Increasing usage pertains to any resource offered by the library from online databases to the most valuable resource in the library, the librarians. Although researchers have expressed a need for more research measuring the effects of ILI on increasing usage, studies on this topic are scarce. The two studies that have been done measured the increases using self-administered surveys by participants. The survey in Figure 2.1 was used in a recent study that measured the effectiveness of ILI in increasing students' usage of the library.

Another behavioral outcome is a change in participant information-seeking behavior. Information-seeking behavior has been of interest to librarians and information science professionals for decades. Although a large number of studies have been done on this subject, the process itself is still largely a mystery and requires more quantitative research.

# Information Literacy Instruction

**Figure 2.1** Library usage questionnaire: pretest/posttest survey

> In the last three weeks, approximately how many times have you
>
> 1. visited the college library?
>    a. None  b. Once  c. 2–3  d. 4–5  e. more than 5
>
> 2. visited the library's webpage or one of the library's databases?
>    a. None  b. Once  c. 2–3  d. 4–5  e. more than 5
>
> 3. accessed the Internet or used other resources to help with your coursework?
>    a. None  b. Once  c. 2–3  d. 4–5  e. more than 5
>
> 4. Have you ever had a library orientation?
>    Yes___          No___

The first model for study of information-seeking behavior was developed by James Krikelas in 1983. This model suggested that the steps of information seeking were as follows: (1) perceiving a need, (2) the search itself, (3) finding the information, and (4) using the information, which results in either satisfaction or dissatisfaction. Krikelas stated that 'information seeking begins when someone perceives that the current state of knowledge is less than that needed to deal with some issue (or problem). The process ends when that perception no longer exists' (Krikelas, 1983). Other models have followed, and included feelings of the searcher, motivation of the participant, cognitive issues, and task definition. Components of the information-seeking process are the need for information, choice of what is relevant information, and the actual information seeking (Algon, 1997). Information-seeking behavior is much more; it consists of the use of information, which includes the absorbing, conceptualizing, manipulating, expressing, and organizing of information (Limberg, 1997). Librarians have long been puzzled by the fact that students seem to be incapable of thinking critically about information needs and through instruction have tried to improve students' information-seeking behavior. Determining changes in information-seeking behavior is not as simple as determining the changes in usage of library resources. Measuring the changes requires extensive and complex questionnaires similar to the example in Figure 2.2.

**Figure 2.2** Questionnaire on information seeking behavior

1. What is your major subject? _____
2. What is the topic of your paper? _____
   _____
3. For how long have you been working on your paper? Mark the right alternative:
   __ 0–6 weeks
   __ 7–12 weeks
4. Have you worked full-time or part-time on your paper? Mark the right alternative:
   __ full-time
   __ part-time
5. In what phase of your paper project are you at the moment? Mark the right alternative (you may choose several alternatives):
   __ developing the research plan __ reading background material
   __ planning the collection of data __ data-collection
   __ analysing the data __ interpreting the results __ final stage
6. What is your average study result? Mark the right alternative:
   ___ satisfactory ___ good ___ excellent

**In the following you will be asked how you use information related to your paper**
Answer the questions on a scale from 1 to 5:
1 false  2 somewhat false  3 neutral  4 somewhat true  5 true

Please note! Avoid alternative 3 unless absolutely necessary.

(*Continued*)

> **Figure 2.2** Questionnaire on information seeking behavior *(cont'd)*

7. The first questions measures cognitive aspects of your information seeking.

7. 1. Articles that are published in journals are reliable
    1 2 3 4 5

7. 2. Many of the studies I have read about were poorly conducted
    1 2 3 4 5

7. 3. I find it easy to see how others could improve their master theses
    1 2 3 4 5

7. 4. What is published in books are facts that can be trusted
    1 2 3 4 5

7. 5. I tend to agree when I hear someone argue for something
    1 2 3 4 5

7. 6. Sometimes I simply do not have time to seek information
    1 2 3 4 5

7. 7. Much of what I have read is written in such a way that it is hard to see what is essential     1 2 3 4 5

7. 8. Most of what I have read for my master thesis agrees with my own opinions     1 2 3 4 5

7. 9. I find it difficult to be critical of what I read     1 2 3 4 5

8. How do you judge whether documents found on the Internet are of good enough quality to be used as references in your paper?
_____

9. What has affected the results in the studies you have read related to your paper?

Rank the following criteria from 1 to 4:

    1 most influential
    2 second influential
    3 third influential
    4 least influential

| | |
|---|---|
| The opinion of the author | 1 2 3 4 |
| The society where the study was done | 1 2 3 4 |
| The method | 1 2 3 4 |
| The phenomenon itself (previous knowledge, investigated item) | 1 2 3 4 |

10. Please mark in percentage how much you think the following criteria affect the way you choose information:

When I search for information for my paper it is important for me to find:

# Objectives of instruction

- only a few documents which exactly match the subject of my thesis
  _____%
- many documents which are at least somewhat related to my thesis
  _____%

The total number should equal 100%

- document = written information like articles, books, web pages, manuals, encyclopedias, newspapers

## Besides the content of a document there may be other criteria which affect the choice of information source.

11. How do you usually judge whether a document fits the topic of your thesis?

Please mark the table:

1 not important
2 of minor importance
3 neutral
4 fairly important
5 important

| | | | | | |
|---|---|---|---|---|---|
| Type of material (if you for instance prefer to read articles over books) | 1 | 2 | 3 | 4 | 5 |
| The appearance of the document (reject a worn-out book or a book in small type) | 1 | 2 | 3 | 4 | 5 |
| It is recently written | 1 | 2 | 3 | 4 | 5 |
| The document seems thorough | 1 | 2 | 3 | 4 | 5 |
| The document gives overview information | 1 | 2 | 3 | 4 | 5 |
| It is written in a clear and plain manner | 1 | 2 | 3 | 4 | 5 |
| The source (for instance the journal) is well-established and known | 1 | 2 | 3 | 4 | 5 |
| The author is respected within his field | 1 | 2 | 3 | 4 | 5 |
| The document is of a high scientific level | 1 | 2 | 3 | 4 | 5 |
| The language of the document | 1 | 2 | 3 | 4 | 5 |

12. Please mark in percentage how much you think the following criteria affect the way you seek information:

When I search for information for my thesis it is important for me to find:

- documents which confirm my own thoughts about the subject
  _____%
- documents which give me new ideas _____%

The total number should equal 100%

(*Continued*)

# Information Literacy Instruction

**Figure 2.2** Questionnaire on information seeking behavior *(cont'd)*

---

13. Please mark in percentage how often you choose:
    - material which brings new perspectives on your field of study
      _____%
    - documents whose contents are recognized and accepted in your field of study _____%

    The total number should equal 100%

14. The following group of questions asks how much you are willing to spend, for instance of your time and money, on your thesis work.

    1 false
    2 somewhat false
    3 neutral
    4 somewhat true
    5 true

    | | | | | | |
    |---|---|---|---|---|---|
    | 14. 1. I use interlibrary loans | 1 | 2 | 3 | 4 | 5 |
    | 14. 2. I am willing to wait more than 2 weeks for an interlibrary loan | 1 | 2 | 3 | 4 | 5 |
    | 14. 3. I am willing to pay for interlibrary loans in order to get the material I need | 1 | 2 | 3 | 4 | 5 |
    | 14. 4. I choose to manage without documents rather than spend much time searching for them | 1 | 2 | 3 | 4 | 5 |
    | 14. 5. I buy books for my thesis | 1 | 2 | 3 | 4 | 5 |
    | 14. 6. It is OK to spend time on information seeking for a master's thesis | 1 | 2 | 3 | 4 | 5 |
    | 14. 7. I am willing to pay for information on the Internet | 1 | 2 | 3 | 4 | 5 |
    | 14. 8. I only use the material which is available in the nearest libraries | 1 | 2 | 3 | 4 | 5 |
    | 14. 9. I prefer to use material which is easily available on the Internet | 1 | 2 | 3 | 4 | 5 |
    | 14. 10. Information seeking is a work and time consuming phase of the thesis work | 1 | 2 | 3 | 4 | 5 |

15. The following questions aim at measuring the way you search for information.

    | | | | | | |
    |---|---|---|---|---|---|
    | 15. 1. In my opinion a small amount of well chosen documents is enough for writing a master's thesis | 1 | 2 | 3 | 4 | 5 |
    | 15. 2. I regularly search for information related to my thesis topic | 1 | 2 | 3 | 4 | 5 |
    | 15. 3. In my opinion it is profitable to concentrate on the first relevant information you find since it saves time | 1 | 2 | 3 | 4 | 5 |

15. 4. In my opinion a large amount of background information is essential before starting a research project                   1 2 3 4 5

15. 5. It is important not to overlook relevant information when seeking for information                   1 2 3 4 5

15. 6. Sometimes I come across information even though I am not consciously looking for it                   1 2 3 4 5

15. 7. I want to find information about all aspects of my thesis subject                   1 2 3 4 5

15. 8. There is a risk of overlooking important information if one does not carefully examine the documents one finds                   1 2 3 4 5

16. Please mark in percentage how true these statements are for you:

How do you react if you search for information in a database and do not get any results on your query?

- Assume nothing is written on the topic _____%
- Continue to search in other databases _____%

The total number should equal 100%

17. When I search for information in a database:

- I plan my searches in advance _____%
- My search is gradually developed. _____%

The total number should equal 100%

18. The last questions ask about the information sources you use.

In the first column, mark the information sources you have used for your thesis.

In the second column, mark the three sources you have used most frequently:

1 most frequently
2 second most frequently
3 third most frequently

Mark the sources you have used 1, 2, 3 for those you have used the most.

I have got information from:

Journals on the Internet   Other material on the Internet   TV
Radio   Encyclopedias   Journals   Books   Newspapers
Teacher, professor   Supervisor   Other students   Friends
Conferences, courses   Brochures, manuals   Presentations, lectures   Associations   Companies   Others (specify)

19. Which of the above sources has been most useful to you and why?

*Source*: Hiensrtom (2002)

Library usage as an effectiveness standard for ILI is perhaps the most logical measurement especially in assessing the one-shot instructional periods. This can be done using a pretest/posttest research design (see Table 2.1). The data can be collected quantitatively or qualitatively. Qualitative collection can be done through interviewing and focus groups. However, this will require a much more significant time commitment and the level of assessment is still programmatic and similar to the results received through surveys. Most institutions require a quantification of the data, they want numbers and statistics, and the qualitative data must be transfigured. Also, the access to the participants will require a greater level of effort than self-administered surveys. Self-administered surveys are most convenient for academic students and can produce accurate measurements.

At the beginning of a semester the pretest surveys (example in Figure 2.1) can be administered to two groups, an experimental group that will receive the instruction and a control group that will receive no instruction. After the experimental group receives instruction, ideally, both groups would be assigned a class project that requires research. Then the experimental group would receive the ILI and the control group would not. An appropriate period of time for research should pass before the posttest surveys are administered to both groups. The pretest surveys must be organized by participants in the posttest survey so the results

**Table 2.1** Pretest/posttest research design

| | | | |
|---|---|---|---|
| Experimental group | Pretest survey administered | Information literacy instruction administered (ILI) | Posttest survey administered |
| Control group | Pretest survey administered | No instruction administered (NI) | Posttest survey administered |

can be recorded correctly. When the surveys are completed the results can be input to a statistical spreadsheet or data form. By using statistical testing ($t$-test and analysis of variance, ANOVA) the changes in the gainscores from the pretest to the posttest results will provide a quantitative measurement for analysis. Using the surveys shown in Figure 2.1 will measure a student's physical and virtual library usage and also determine how often they have used other Internet resources. Information-seeking behavior can be measured using the same research design as the questionnaire in Figure 2.2. This type of survey demands more commitment from the student and may require other extrinsic rewards to influence participation. The statistical testing requirements include a $t$-test, a factor analysis, a Pearson Regression, and a stepwise regression to determine the changes from pretest to posttest (Hiensrtom, 2002). The instrumentation and testing are more complex and the research study is more time intensive for determining information-seeking behavioral changes. However, it is certainly worth the extra work if this is the effectiveness standard of the program. Other than increasing usage, the most basic goal of library instruction is to influence students' information-seeking skills, and scientific research is the most effective assessment of both these behavioral outcomes.

Behavioral outcomes are an excellent method for measuring the effectiveness of an ILI program. There are countless studies linking library usage with academic achievement and the results confirm that students who use the library have higher reading and academic scores. Usage statistics justify a library's existence and are what directors use for budget justification. An ILI program that scientifically proves that it increases usage of the library or is capable of improving a student's information-seeking skills needs no other determining factor for success.

## Cognitive outcomes

In the mid-1980s, as the concept of information literacy began to develop, the assessment movement began emerging. It was no surprise that these two movements crossed paths, as accountability became an increasing concern on college campuses (NPEC, 2005). The assessment movement has grown, and assessing student learning has become a priority focus in higher education. The expansion of ILI in academic libraries has paralleled the growth of assessment, and if academic libraries want to remain relevant on university campuses they must show how they are contributing to the process of improving student learning. The most influential way they have done this is through using cognitive outcomes as an effectiveness standard for ILI.

Cognitive outcomes are changes in knowledge of participants and deal with information-processing habits. They relate to how people observe, think, problem solve and remember, and describe how people perceive, organize, and retain information (Grassian and Kaplowitz, 2009). They show what students have learned from the instruction, and the cognitive skills related to ILI include identifying necessary information, extracting the required information, evaluating information critically, and using information from a wide range of resources. The Association of College and Research Libraries has developed a set of competencies for higher education that were subsequently endorsed by the American Association for Higher Education. The five basic competencies for information literacy as they appear in ACRL's publication, *Information Literacy Competency Standards for Higher Education* (2000), are listed below:

- The information literate student determines the nature and extent of the information needed.

- The information literate student accesses needed information effectively and efficiently.
- The information literate student evaluates information and its sources critically and incorporates selected information into his or her knowledge base and value system.
- The information literate student, individually or as a member of a group, uses information effectively to accomplish a specific purpose.
- The information literate student understands many of the economic, legal, and social issues surrounding the use of information, and accesses and uses information ethically and legally. (ACRL, 2000)

Changes in cognitive outcomes can be as small as remembering the high points of what was taught to applying what was taught to a real life situation and may require more than a simple survey to collect results. Many academic libraries assess their ILI programs by applying Bloom's taxonomy of educational objectives (as revised by Anderson and Krathwohl) to determine the level of cognitive learning outcomes listed in the ACRL competencies.

Table 2.2 shows the revised Bloom taxonomy created by Anderson and Krathwohl. The revised taxonomy is more suited to determining the level of cognitive learning outcomes than the original because the new updates incorporate new knowledge into the taxonomy framework.

As indicated in Figure 2.3, the visual layout of the levels shows a conversion from the original noun levels to the verb levels of the revised structure. This transformation from noun to verb use allows the levels to be laid out with the levels of knowledge, making it easy to match activities and objectives to the types of knowledge for assessment purposes.

Table 2.3 illustrates a cross-impact grid matching the cognitive processes with types of knowledge and includes a definition of the knowledge dimensions.

Information literacy skills can be applied to the different levels of learning in Bloom's taxonomy. Two scholars from the University of Worcester, Massachusetts, Dr Judith Keene

**Table 2.2** The revised Bloom taxonomy

| Bloom's taxonomy 1956 | Anderson and Krathwohl's taxonomy 2000 |
|---|---|
| 1. Knowledge: Remembering or retrieving previously learned material. Examples of verbs that relate to this function are:<br>know    define    record<br>recall    identify    name<br>memorize    relate    recognize<br>repeat    list    acquire | 1. Remembering: Retrieving, recalling, or recognizing knowledge from memory. Remembering is when memory is used to produce definitions, facts, or lists, or to recite or retrieve material. |
| 2. Comprehension: The ability to grasp or construct meaning from material. Examples of verbs that relate to this function are:<br>restate    identify    discuss<br>locate    review    infer<br>report    illustrate    interpret<br>recognize    draw    represent<br>explain    differentiate    express<br>discuss    conclude | 2. Understanding: Constructing meaning from different types of functions, be they written or graphic messages. It includes activities like interpreting, exemplifying, classifying, summarizing, inferring, comparing, and explaining. |
| 3. Application: The ability to use learned material, or to implement material in new and concrete situations. Examples of verbs that relate to this function are:<br>apply    organize    practice<br>relate    employ    calculate<br>develop    restructure    show<br>translate    interpret    exhibit<br>use    demonstrate    dramatize<br>operate    illustrate | 3. Applying: Carrying out or using a procedure through executing or implementing. Applying related and refers to situations where learned material is used through products like models, presentations, interviews or simulations. |

# Objectives of instruction

4. Analysis: The ability to break down or distinguish the parts of material into its components so that its organizational structure may be better understood. Examples of verbs that relate to this function are:

| | | |
|---|---|---|
| analyze | differentiate | experiment |
| compare | contrast | scrutinize |
| probe | investigate | discover |
| inquire | detect | inspect |
| examine | survey | dissect |
| contrast | classify | discriminate |
| categorize | deduce | separate |

4. Analyzing: Breaking material or concepts into parts, determining how the parts relate or interrelate to one another or to an overall structure or purpose. Mental actions included in this function are differentiating, organizing, and attributing, as well as being able to distinguish between the components or parts. When one is analyzing one can illustrate this mental function by creating spreadsheets, surveys, charts, diagrams, or graphic representations.

5. Synthesis: The ability to put parts together to form a coherent or unique new whole. Examples of verbs that relate to this function are:

| | | |
|---|---|---|
| compose | plan | develop |
| produce | invent | arrange |
| design | formulate | construct |
| assemble | collect | organize |
| create | set up | originate |
| prepare | generalize | derive |
| predict | document | write |
| modify | combine | propose |
| tell | relate | |

5. Evaluating: Making judgments based on criteria and standards through checking and critiquing. Critiques, recommendations, and reports are some of the products that can be created to demonstrate the processes of evaluation. In the newer taxonomy evaluation comes before creating as it is often a necessary part of the precursory behavior before creating something.

Remember this one has now changed places with the last one on the other side.

*(Continued)*

73

# Information Literacy Instruction

**Table 2.2** The revised Bloom taxonomy (cont'd)

| Bloom's taxonomy 1956 | Anderson and Krathwohl's taxonomy 2000 |
|---|---|
| 6. Evaluation: The ability to judge, check, and even critique the value of material for a given purpose. Examples of verbs that relate to this function are:<br>judge     argue     validate<br>assess    decide    consider<br>compare   choose    appraise<br>evaluate  rate      value<br>conclude  select    criticize<br>measure   estimate  infer<br>deduce | 6. Creating: Putting elements together to form a coherent or functional whole; reorganizing elements into a new pattern or structure through generating, planning, or producing. Creating requires users to put parts together in a new way or synthesize parts into something new and different – a new form or product. This process is the most difficult mental function in the new taxonomy.<br><br>This one used to be #5 in Bloom's synthesis. |

*Source*: Anderson and Krathwohl (2001).

**Figure 2.3** Levels of cognitive learning

| Bloom et al., 1956 | Anderson and Krathwohl, 2000 |
|---|---|

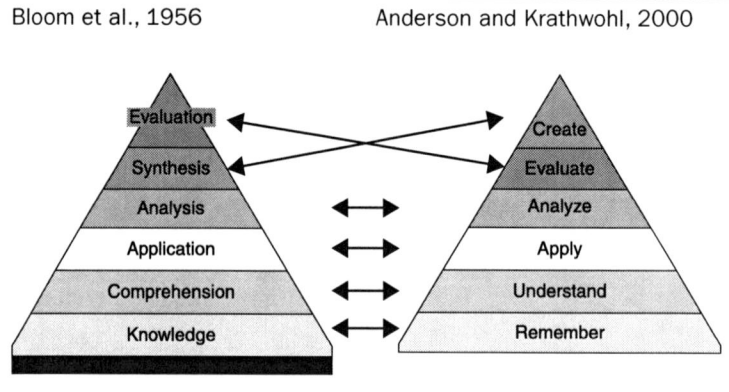

*Source*: Anderson and Krathwohl (2001).

### Table 2.3  Cross-impact grid

| Cognitive processes | | | | | | |
|---|---|---|---|---|---|---|
| The Knowledge Dimensions | 1 Remember | 2 Understand | 3 Apply | 4 Analyze | 5 Evaluate | 6 Create |
| Factual | | | | | | |
| Conceptual | | | | | | |
| Procedural | | | | | | |
| Metacognitive | | | | | | |

Source: Anderson and Krathwohl (2001).

**Knowledge dimensions defined:**
Factual knowledge is knowledge that is basic to specific disciplines. This dimension refers to essential facts, terminology, details, or elements students must know or be familiar with in order to understand a discipline or solve a problem in it.
Conceptual knowledge is knowledge of classifications, principles, generalizations, theories, models, or structures pertinent to a particular disciplinary area.
Procedural knowledge refers to information or knowledge that helps students to do something specific to a discipline, subject, area of study. It also refers to methods of inquiry, very specific or finite skills, algorithms, techniques, and particular methodologies.
Metacognitive knowledge is the awareness of one's own cognition and particular cognitive processes. It is strategic or reflective knowledge about how to go about solving problems, cognitive tasks, to include contextual and conditional knowledge and knowledge of self.

and John Colvin, have designed a model of information literacy that maps the activities that students undertake while learning information literacy skills. The model maps the activities against the cognitive skill levels of Bloom's taxonomy. Each stage of information literacy is matched up with the cognitive skills required to learn the IL skill. Table 2.4 uses the structure of the Colvin-Keene (CK) Model to define the cognitive skills employed in each of the four stages of information literacy. Colvin and Keene use the original Bloom taxonomy terms, and Table 2.4

**Table 2.4** Information literacy and cognitive skills

| Stages of information literacy | Bloom's revised cognitive skills |
| --- | --- |
| Information needs identification stage (ACRL Competency 1) | Remember (Knowledge, original Bloom skills)<br>Understand (comprehension)<br>Apply (application)<br>Analyze (analysis) |
| Information location and evaluation (ACRL Competency 2) | Remember (knowledge)<br>Understand (comprehension)<br>Apply (application) |
| Information review (ACRL Competency 3) | Remember (knowledge)<br>Understand (comprehension)<br>Analyze (analysis)<br>Evaluate (evaluation) |
| Problem solution (ACRL Competency 4 and 5) | Remember (knowledge)<br>Apply (application)<br>Evaluate (evaluation)<br>Create (synthesis) |

*Source*: Keene, Colvin and Sissons (2010)

substitutes the revised verb terms defined by Anderson and Krathwohl.

The first stage identifies the information need and requires the student to employ different cognitive skills to advance to the next stage or competency in the cycle. A student must analyze an introduced problem, for example a class assignment requiring a research paper, and remember, understand, and apply possessed information to identify the information need. The next stage of access and evaluation of information also requires multiple cognitive skills to proceed. A student must remember, understand, and apply previous knowledge to locate, evaluate, and retrieve appropriate resources to fulfill the information need identified in stage one. In stage three the student critically analyzes the found resources and identifies the relevant information that can be used to solve the problem, summarizing pertinent facts for use. Stage four also employs multiple skills as the student synthesizes the information to solve the problem using citations and writing styles. In comparison to the presentation of the linear design ACRL Competencies, the CK Model presents information literacy as a cycle (Keene, Colvin, and Sissons, 2010). Both designs emphasize always improving information literacy skills, but the CK Model defines the information literacy process that a student goes through while completing a research assignment (see Figure 2.4). The ACRL Competencies address every facet of information literacy (Keene, Colvin, and Sissons, 2010). The cycle of completing a research assignment employs every cognitive skill of information literacy. The Colvin-Keene cyclical design 'emphasizes the relevant cognitive skills exercised by students at each stage of the information cycle' (Keene, Colvin, and Sissons, 2010). This parallel pattern makes Colvin-Keene a more realistic approach to apply to instructional design of ILI programs in academic libraries.

Accreditation is the most important factor in determining a college's or university's academic credibility, and all accreditation agencies have made information literacy a required standard. They have defined the importance of the relationship between information literacy and student learning outcomes. As information literacy has become an important aspect of higher education, the need exists for authentic assessment models to identify learning outcomes in academic library instructional programs. Though there have been increases in measuring the effectiveness of ILI programs, more work needs to be done on measuring the effectiveness of ILI in increasing cognitive outcomes. There are different approaches to assessing this. Measuring cognitive outcomes can occur at any point in the instructional process, before, during, or after. Alternatively, it is done most effectively using a research design similar to the illustration in Table 2.1.

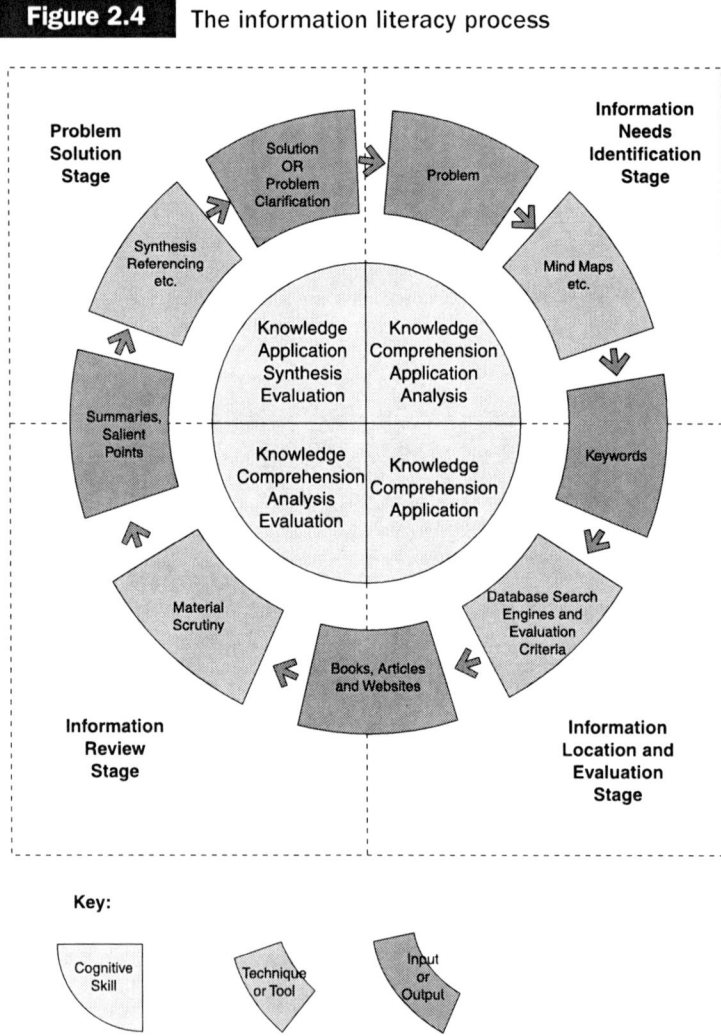

**Figure 2.4** The information literacy process

Pretest participants in groups that receive the instruction and groups that do not, administer the instruction, and posttest both groups. There are also different measurement instruments. Comparable to measuring behavioral outcomes, interviews and focus groups can be used, though the same limitations apply. Knowledge tests and performance assessments are most commonly used, and both can provide effective and accurate results.

Knowledge tests and performance assessments developed in-house can require enormous resources, and many institutions consider ready-made solutions. Standardized information literacy tests have been developed by some prominent organizations and are designed to measure many different standards including the ACRL *Information Literacy Competency Standards of Higher Education*. The tests come in a variety of forms and levels, including measurements of real-life experiences that will determine a more 'authentic assessment experience' (Grassian and Kaplowitz, 2009). Figure 2.5 presents a list of standardized tests created by a professor of psychology at North Central College in Illinois, Jon Mueller. The list provides the name of the test and the institution that created the test, and includes a short description. The list includes two tutorial resources with embedded assessment that measures student learning in the course of the instruction (Mueller, 2010). Many similar tutorials can be found on the Internet.

Sue Samson, a Professor and Head, Information and Research Services at the Mansfield Library of the University of Montana, recently developed an effectiveness measuring instrument for the Mansfield Library instructional program. It is a standardized test that quantifies cognitive learning outcomes and is based on the ACRL *Standards*. Like many measurement instruments, Samson bases assessment on a completed research assignment or paper. Papers of a group of students who received instruction are collected and analyzed. Based on the ACRL *Standards*, the instrument assesses the performance indicators of each of five standards with quantifiable measures. Table 2.5 shows how the test measures each standard, with a list of questions used to quantify some of the competencies (Samson, 2010). The

# Information Literacy Instruction

**Figure 2.5** List of standardized knowledge tests

**Forced-choice tests (e.g., multiple-choice, true/false)**

**Student information literacy survey** – from Texas Lutheran University – 25 multiple-choice questions

**Information literacy assessment** – from University of La Verne Wilson Library – 18 multiple-choice questions

**Information literacy assessment** – from Carl Albert State College – 10 multiple-choice questions

**Sports medicine information literacy test** – from West Chester University – 12 multiple-choice questions

**Information literacy questionnaire** – from the Conference of Rectors and Principals of Quebec Universities – 16 multiple-choice questions – starts on p. 79 of this long document – a version in French follows the English version

**Beile test of information literacy** – developed by Penny Beile

**Information literacy assessment** – from Madonna University Library, pre- and post-tests

**Information literacy assessment** – from UW-Whitewater, University Library – 9 multiple-choice questions

**Information literacy quiz** – from Bellevue Community College – 21 multiple-choice and true/false questions – also find a variety of discipline-specific assessments and activities

**TRAILS (Tools for Real-time Assessment of Information Literacy Skills)** – from Kent State University – 'There are two general assessments (30 items each), as well as two 10-item assessments in each of the five categories (Develop Topic; Identify Potential Sources; Develop, Use, and Revise Search Strategies; Evaluate Sources and Information; Recognize How to Use Information Responsibly, Ethically, and Legally). The assessment pairs are parallel in terms of concepts addressed and may be used as pre- and post-tests.' – Free for use by library media specialists and teachers

**SAILS (Standardized Assessment of Information Literacy Skills)** – also from Kent State University – SAILS is a 45-item multiple-choice, college-level test aligned with the ACRL Information Literacy Competency Standards for Higher Education. 'Students are directed to the SAILS web site to take the web-based test. Each student

# Objectives of instruction

may take the test once per administration. Responses are sent to a central database where data are analyzed and reports are generated and made available for download in PDF.' 'The SAILS test asks students questions about research strategies; selecting sources; understanding and using finding tools; developing and revising search strategies; evaluating results; retrieving materials; documenting sources; and legal and social issues related to ethical and effective use of information. The test identifies areas where students have strong information literacy skills and where skills need to be strengthened.' There is a per-student fee for participation.

**Information competency assessment instrument** – from California State University, Dominguez Hills – 27 multiple-choice questions

**Test your research skills** – from Raritan Valley Community College/Evelyn S. Field Library – 25 multiple-choice questions

**NetTrail Quiz** – from the University of California Santa Cruz – 17 multiple-choice questions

**Information literacy assessment** – from Ann Viles, Appalachian State University – 28 multiple-choice questions

## Authentic assessments (see *Authentic Assessment Toolbox*)

**Portfolio assessment** – from Teesside University – description of portfolio assignments can be found in the appendix of this article, beginning on p. 32

**Information literacy skills survey** – from the Plano (Texas) Independent School District – a series of fill-in-the-blank and short essay questions for the middle school level

**LILO (Learning Information Literacy Online)** Tutorial plus Rubrics – from the University of Hawai'i Libraries – The first link takes you to an online tutorial that can be used as part of a course or completed independently. A nice feature of the tutorial is that you can have students complete journal entries associated with specific information literacy skills in response to specific prompts. Those journal entries can then be evaluated with the rubrics found at the second link.

**Information literacy quiz** – from November Learning, a company that provides a variety of development services – includes 13 brief essay questions – also includes answers to quiz and some possible follow-up activities

(*Continued*)

# Information Literacy Instruction

**Figure 2.5** List of standardized knowledge tests (*cont'd*)

Information literacy assessment – from Rappahannock Community College – a 'research log' assignment in which students answer questions about a research assignment just completed – apparently, meant less as a summative assessment to evaluate students and more as a formative assessment to provide feedback for instruction

Information literacy assessment – from Pasadena City College (adapted from following assessment by Topsy Smalley) – contains nine constructed-response or short essay questions

Information literacy assessment – from Topsy Smalley at Cabrillo College – contains nine constructed-response or short essay questions

Information literacy and research skills course assessments – from Minneapolis Community and Technical College – An excellent and extensive set of authentic assignments and tests that accompany this course on Information Literacy and Research Skills from the Library and Information Studies faculty. On this page you can find links to several information literacy assignments with their accompanying (and detailed) rubrics. Additionally, you can find take-home mid-term and final exams that require students to apply these skills. Finally, there is a link to a research portfolio and accompanying rubric that can be used across disciplines. Oh wait, there's more . . . but I'll let you explore.

Assessing student learning outcomes – from Dana Franks at Highline Community College – scroll down page to find assessment which is a group activity in which students select a topic, complete a 'Great Finds' task, and give a group presentation – detailed rubrics are included

Alternative research assignments – from Stauffer Library, Queen's University, Kingston, Ontario – a good list of authentic assessment tasks

**Blended assessments (some combination of forced-choice and constructed-response or performance items)**

Information literacy assessment – from the Network of Illinois Learning Resources in Community Colleges – 'The instrument consists of approximately 40 questions. There is a survey of library use attitudes, drawn (with the author's permission) from Carol Kulthau's book, Seeking Meaning. (See More Information Literacy Resources.) In addition to multiple choice questions, there are several open-ended questions. Several of these constructed-response questions are follow-ups to "yes/no" questions. We found that these constructed responses, while not scored, provide valuable insight into how students seek, find and use information.' **You will have to login with the provided ID and password to view the assessment.**

**Bay Area Community Colleges information competency assessment** – includes 47 multiple-choice, matching, and short-answer items and 12 performance exercises – see detailed rubrics

## Rubrics

**Information literacy rubric** – from Palm Beach State College

**Information literacy rubrics** – from West Chester University

**Information literacy portfolio rubric** – from the New Jersey Institute of Technology

**Information literacy rubric** – from the New Jersey City University

**Cited references rubric** – from the University of Central Florida

**Rubric for assessing research papers** – from Merz, Lawrie H. and Beth L. Mark, comp. Assessment in College Library Instruction Programs (CLIP Note #32). Chicago: Association of College and Research Libraries, College Libraries Section, 2002.

**Information literacy rubric** – School Library New York State

**Information literacy rubric** – from St. John's University

**Information literacy rubric** – from Utah State University

**Information literacy rubric for general education** – from Augustana College

**Rubrics for the assessment of information literacy** – from Colorado Department of Education, State Library and Adult Education Office, Colorado Educational Media Association (scroll down page to find rubrics)

## Tutorials

**The Libraries at Washington State University** has a long list of internally developed information literacy tutorials.

**Texas Lutheran University** also has a long list of tutorials, collected by Mark Dibble.

*Source*: Mueller (2010)

**Table 2.5** Measuring ACRL competency standards

| ACRL competency standard | Measurement |
| --- | --- |
| Standard one: The information literate student determines the nature and extent of the information needed | Types and number of sources and formats used by students in the bibliographies of their research papers. |
| Standard two: The information literate student accesses needed information effectively and efficiently | Quantify by the following questions:<br>■ Is there evidence that a database has been used?<br>■ Which database(s)?<br>■ Is there evidence that Google Scholar has been used?<br>■ Is there evidence that interlibrary loan may have been used?<br>■ Is there evidence that the student has collected his/her own research for the project?<br>■ Describe the nature and extent of that research. |
| Standard three: The information literate student evaluates information and its sources critically and incorporates selected information into his or her knowledge base and value system | The ability to evaluate and incorporate information is identified by the contextual application of sources into the research based on the following questions:<br>■ How many short direct quotes (three lines or less) are included in the text?<br>■ How many long direct quotes (four lines or more) are included in the text?<br>■ How many total in-text citations are included in the essay?<br>■ Are the quotes used as filler?<br>■ Does the author acknowledge, question, or combat possible author or publication bias in the essay?<br>■ How does the student accomplish this?<br>■ Does the author connect sources to their cultural context? |

# Objectives of instruction

| | |
|---|---|
| | ■ How does the student accomplish this? |
| | ■ Does the author create an original thesis statement using the supporting evidence he/she presents? |
| | ■ Does the author offer a new hypothesis in his/her paper that may need to be tested in further studies? |
| | ■ Does the author investigate different viewpoints offered in the literature? |
| Standard four: The information literate student, individually or as a member of a group, uses information effectively to accomplish a specific purpose | Attempts to capture the effective use of information are quantified with three questions: |
| | ■ Does the student organize the content in a manner that supports the purposes and format of the product or performance? |
| | ■ Does the student maintain a journal or log of activities related to the information seeking, evaluating, and communicating processes? |
| | ■ Does the student reflect on past successes, failures, and alternative strategies? |
| Standard five: The information literate student understands many of the economic, legal, and social issues surrounding the use of information and accesses and uses information ethically and legally | Quantify student understanding of using information ethically and legally with these two questions: |
| | ■ Does the student select an appropriate documentation style and use it consistently to cite sources? |
| | ■ Does the student post permission granted notices, as needed, for copyrighted material? |

results of the test need to be recorded and input into a statistical software for analysis. The method has been scientifically proven to be a valid and accurate test for measuring cognitive outcomes of students.

There are many advantages to using cognitive outcomes as an effectiveness standard, and standardized testing can be beneficial beyond measuring the effectiveness of your program. They offer an answer to making information literacy assessment a foundational element of the educational process within higher education. Grassian and Kaplowitz claim 'many educators and librarians are looking toward these tools as possible ways to have IL assessment become a standard part of our educational system' (Grassian and Kaplowitz, 2009). Results of the tests can be used in many ways to advance the library. The tests can be used as input measures before students enter a certain level of education or class and as indicators of progress toward a major or a graduation competency, and are a good measurement instrument to test the long term impact of ILI programs (Grassian and Kaplowitz, 2009).

## *Affective outcomes*

The promotion of the importance of assessing cognitive outcomes has overshadowed the need for measuring the affective outcomes of ILI, and these types of outcomes have largely gone unnoticed throughout higher education. Robert Schroeder and Ellysa Cahoy are two members of the committee responsible for revising the ACRL Information Literacy Competency Standards for Higher Education document. They claim 'higher education information literacy standards have readily addressed cognitive skills, although affective competencies – the emotional abilities that students must acquire in order to successfully navigate the research process – have not yet been incorporated into standards' (Schroeder and Cahoy, 2010). The lack of attention most likely stems from the difficulty in codifying and measuring affective outcomes. Schroeder and Cahoy believe defining affective outcomes can be confusing and elusive, writing, 'by its very nature, the realm of affect is more ambiguous, less logical, and less clearly defined than the cognitive domain' (Schroeder and Cahoy, 2010). Table 2.6 lists a set of terms collected by Schroeder and Cahoy used to describe the concept of affective outcomes. From these terms Schroeder and Cahoy have formulated this working definition: 'The affective domain comprises a person's attitudes, emotions, interests, motivation, self-efficacy, and values' (Schroeder and Cahoy, 2010). The challenges of measuring affective outcomes may derive from the fact that they involve a student's behavior and confidence level toward learning something before and after instruction – not how well they

**Table 2.6** Terms associated with the concept of affect by various authors

| | | |
|---|---|---|
| Attitudes | Attitudes | Attitudes |
| Interests | Beliefs | Beliefs |
| Sentiments | Emotions | Interests |
| Values | Perceptions | Openness |
| | Psychosocial responses or behaviors | Needs |
| | | Opinions |
| | Sensations | Personal temperament |
| | Values | Social temperament |
| | | Values |
| Jum C. Nunally | William J. Gephart | Ralph Hoepfner |
| Activities | Attitudes | Appreciations |
| Assumptions | Attitudes about self | Biases |
| Attitudes | Attributions | Degree of acceptance or rejection |
| Beliefs and convictions | Continuing motivation | Emotion |
| Feelings | Emotions | Emotional sets |
| Goals or purposes | Feelings | Feeling tone |
| Interests | Interest | Interests |
| Worries, problems, obstacles | Morals and ethics | Values |
| | Self-development | |
| | Social competence | |
| | Values | |
| Louis Edward Raths | Barbara L. Martin | David Krathwohl |

Source: Schroeder and Cahoy, 2010

have learned from instruction. Measuring affective outcomes is a different, more psychological approach than evaluating the effectiveness of ILI and has to do with personal feelings an individual has toward a particular experience. Affective experiences refer to a person's emotional reactions that he or she experiences during task performance (Ren, 2000). The two most common experiences related to task performance using library skills are self-efficacy and library anxiety. ILI is used to increase participants' self-efficacy and decrease library anxiety.

## Self-efficacy

Self-efficacy refers to an individual's belief in having the required skills to perform a given task (Cassidy and Eachus, 1997). Noted social psychologist Albert Bandura defined it as 'a belief in one's own capabilities to organize and execute the course of action required to attain a goal' (Bandura, 1998). It is the confidence one has in doing something, and it is the foundation of motivation for just about everything humans do (Kurbanoglu, 2009). If a person believes they cannot do something, there is very little incentive to act or persist in completing a task. Bandura believes that possession of the necessary skills only fulfills half the requirements in completing a given task. He claims that an individual must also have the self-confidence to use the skills effectively in order to successfully complete the task (Bandura, 1997; Kurbanoglu, 2009). Low levels of self-efficacy will most likely lead to failure, when the individual believes the task is insurmountable and has no ambition to continue. However, individuals with a high level of self-efficacy in a certain skill will continue at a challenging task, anticipating eventual success, and persist until they succeed. Serap Kurbanoglu, an information management professor at Hacettepe University in Ankara, Turkey, claims that besides learning information literacy skills, individuals in today's societies must also develop confidence in the skills that they are learning. Many of today's students lack self-efficacy when confronted with using library resources. They do not see library resources, especially electronic databases, as being straightforward or easy to use. They are used to Internet search engines such as Google and when confronted by failures in their search strategies using library databases, usually give up (Waldman, 2003). Karbanoglu writes, 'attainment of a strong sense of self-efficacy beliefs becomes as important as possessing information literacy skills' (Kurbanoglu, 2009). Students who believe they can access and use information effectively will do so effectively.

Though the study of the effects of ILI on self-efficacy is limited, the research has shown that information literacy instructional sessions are effective in improving students' self-efficacy in using the library and its resources (Martin, 1989; Ren, 2000; Nahl-Jakobovitz, 1993). A study performed by Wen-Hau Ren, a librarian at Rutgers University in New Jersey, showed a significant increase in student self-efficacy in using the library's electronic databases after instruction. In an article describing her study she writes, 'This study shows that college students' self-efficacy in electronic information searching was significantly higher after library instruction' (Ren, 2000). The effectiveness of the instruction was measured with pre- and posttest surveys. The surveys contained four sections: (1) self-efficacy in using library electronic sources; (2) attitudes toward acquiring online search skills; (3) use frequency of computer, e-mail, the Internet, and library electronic databases; and (4) individual background information. The posttest survey questionnaire was filled out by the students after they submitted the library assignment. The second questionnaire contained the same first two sections in the preinstruction questionnaire.

Additionally, it asked the participants to assess their electronic searching performance and report any negative emotions experienced when completing the assignment. Thirteen tasks/skills were listed in regard to searching the library online catalog, online periodical databases, and the library's website. Students were asked how confident they were at performing each task and confidence levels were rated on a 10 point scale, with 1 being not confident and 10 being very confident. Students were also asked to self-assess their own searching performance as well as being evaluated by a librarian. Results determined that the instruction was not only effective at increasing the students' technical skills, it also cultivated and improved the self-efficacy of the students, increasing learning outcomes.

A similar 2005 study carried out at the University of Central Florida confirmed the effectiveness of ILI in increasing students' self-efficacy. Two UCF librarians, Jenny Beile and David Boote, conducted research comparing web-based instruction with face-to-face instruction and found that, regardless of the method, self-efficacy levels increased across all groups (Beile and Boote, 2005). The effectiveness was measured by surveys that evaluated self-efficacy (see Figure 2.6). 'Self-efficacy scores were determined by responses on a library skills self-efficacy scale. Participants responded to statements such as, 'I can identify equivalent or related search terms', and 'I can search for books by author in the library catalog', or 'I can easily differentiate between primary and secondary resources by indicating how strongly they agreed with the statement on a 5-point Likert-type scale, ranging from 1 (strongly disagree) to 5 (strongly agree)' (Beile and Boote, 2005). An analysis of the results showed a significant improvement in self-efficacy levels and proved that repeated exposure to ILI offers even more positive effects on self-efficacy levels. The researchers suggested that, within the context of library skills, increased levels of self-efficacy are positively related to greater learning outcomes. These findings are consistent with other studies measuring the effectiveness of instruction in increasing self-efficacy levels and the increases having a positive correlation with increasing student learning outcomes. As mentioned, measuring affective outcomes such as increases in self-efficacy levels can be difficult; however, as Beile and Boote recommend in their discussion, 'these and other similar findings suggest librarians would do well to attend to the affective domain as well as the cognitive' (Beile and Boote, 2005). Self-efficacy is an individual's belief in the ability to perform a given task. Bandura's self-efficacy research showed that individuals' belief systems affect their behaviors and how much they are willing to do to succeed in the information-seeking process. Self-efficacy is a predictor of research achievement (Mellon, 1986) and should be considered an important alternative approach when evaluating the effectiveness of ILI.

## Library anxiety

Library anxiety is common among college students and is characterized by feelings of inadequacy and negative emotions including tension, fear, and mental disorganization (Jiao and Onwuegbuzie, 1999). It is not mutually exclusive to college students and academic libraries. In fact, when faced with using library resources to fulfill information needs, most people in all types of libraries suffer from confusion and uncertainty, especially with a difficult, complex information-seeking assignment (Battle, 2004). Constance Mellon, a library science professor at the University of North Carolina, was the first to identify and define students' apprehension in using the library as library anxiety. She described it as an uncomfortable feeling or emotional disposition experienced in a library setting that has cognitive, affective, physiological, and behavioral ramifications (Mellon, 1986). Library anxiety has foundations in self-efficacy and is due to students' belief that they do not possess the required skills to complete a research assignment. It can have a damaging effect on student learning and a long-term harmful effect on a student's academic career. Most often the anxious feelings develop from intimidation at the size and complexity of the library. The library's resources do not seem to be as friendly and intuitive as the commercial search engines that students are familiar with. Other common causes stem from student unpreparedness and the increasing non-traditional and international element of current student populations. There has been much research conducted in the field since Mellon's identification and most results show the best intervention for reducing students anxiety is ILI (Onwuegbuzie et al., 2004).

The most effective way to reduce library anxiety is to first identify the students who are experiencing anxiety, then have them attend library instructional sessions that emphasize affective skills development and search strategies (Jiao and Onwuegbuzie, 1997). Sharon Bostick, a former director of the University of Massachusetts, Boston Library, identified five different antecedents of library anxiety, namely barriers with staff, affective barriers, comfort with the library, knowledge of the library, and mechanical barriers. In the early 1990s she developed a measuring tool to determine levels of anxiety in students called the Library Anxiety Scale (LAS). The LAS has been the only widely used instrument to measure library anxiety. The LAS is a 43 item, 5 point Likert type format which measures levels of library anxiety. The 43 items are grouped into the 5 antecedents used to determine what barriers are causing a student's anxiety. Figure 2.6 shows the 43 questions, each followed by the numbers 1–5, with 1 meaning 'Strongly disagree' and 5 'Strongly agree'. Bostick claims the fact that this is the only instrument to date to be utilized in measuring library anxiety suggests that other measuring standards are needed to incorporate the expansion of environments. She writes, 'The most significant changes in the library and information field during the last decade have been the transition from location-specific information environments to the more open, virtual information settings' (Onwuegbuzie, Jiao and Bostick, 2004). New questions should attempt to determine a participant's level of comfort with electronic environments, including use of web-based resources and other computerized aspects of research. Onwuegbuzie, Jiao and Bostick suggest researchers also need to administer the scale at specific times relevant to a participant's highest anxiety levels, such as just after an assignment is given to the student and before the research is started. They suggest this type of intervention before research starts will contribute to the outcomes and provide a more accurate measurement of anxiety before and after library use.

The task of measuring affective outcomes has proved to be very challenging to researchers. Though it seems to be one of the most appropriate measures of effectiveness, few researchers have attempted to measure students' thoughts and feelings about using the library. This pattern must change; self-efficacy and library anxiety are most likely the greatest deterrents of library use. Reducing anxiety and increasing participant confidence in their library skills should be written as goals and objectives of every academic library instructional program (Kurbanogul, 2009). Measuring levels of anxiety and efficacy will help identify students who require the most assistance. Academic librarians need to define new

# Information Literacy Instruction

**Figure 2.6** The Library Anxiety Scale

1. _____ I am embarrassed that I don't know how to use the library.
2. _____ A lot of the university is confusing to me.
3. _____ The librarians are unapproachable.
4. _____ The reference librarians are unhelpful.
5. _____ The librarians don't have time to help me because they're always on the telephone.
6. _____ I can't get help in the library at the times I need it.
7. _____ Library clerks don't have time to help me.
8. _____ The reference librarians don't have time to help me because they're always busy doing something else.
9. _____ I am unsure about how to begin my research.
10. _____ I get confused trying to find my way around the library.
11. _____ I don't know what to do next when the book I need is not on the shelf.
12. _____ The reference librarians are not approachable.
13. _____ I enjoy, learning new things about the library.
14. _____ If I can't find a book on the shelf the library staff will help me.
15. _____ There is often no one available in the library to help me.
16. _____ I feel comfortable using the library.
17. _____ I feel like I'm bothering the reference librarian if I ask a question.
18. _____ I feel safe in the library.
19. _____ I feel comfortable in the library.
20. _____ The reference librarians are unfriendly.
21. _____ I can always ask a librarian if I don't know how to work a piece of equipment in the library.
22. _____ The library is a comfortable place to study.
23. _____ The library never has the materials I need.
24. _____ I can never find things in the library.
25. _____ There is too much crime in the library.
26. _____ The people who work at the circulation desk are helpful.
27. _____ The library staff doesn't care about students.
28. _____ The library is an important part of my school.
29. _____ I want to learn to do my own research.
30. _____ The copy machines are usually out of order.
31. _____ I don't understand the library's overdue fines.
32. _____ Good instructions for using the library's computers are available.
33. _____ Librarians don't have time to help me.
34. _____ The library's rules are too restrictive.
35. _____ I don't feel physically safe in the library.
36. _____ The computer printers are often out of paper.
37. _____ The directions for using the computers are not clear.
38. _____ I don't know what resources are available in the library.
39. _____ The library staff doesn't listen to students.
40. _____ The change machines are usually out of order.
41. _____ The library is a safe place.
42. _____ The library won't let me check out as many items as I need.
43. _____ I can't find enough space in the library to study.

*Source*: LAS designed by Sharon Bostick in 1992, cited from Onwuegbuzie, Jiao and Bostick (2004).

methods that are effective in measuring anxiety and efficacy and new instructional methods that reduce the former and increase the latter.

## Take-home message

This chapter defined the different categories an ILI program can use to determine its success and effectiveness. Whether measuring behavioral, cognitive, or affective outcomes, remember that all assessment is beneficial to the library and its participants. Assessing instructional effectiveness by measuring outcomes is vitally important to the success of a library's instructional program. It is the best way to determine the effectiveness of the program and it can help improve an instructional program. Assessment can expose areas not contributing to the advancement of student learning and areas that do not support the library's goals. Increased library use denotes increased student learning, less anxiety promotes use, and students having the confidence to do it on their own increases learning skills. Measuring effectiveness can point a library in the right direction. Grassian and Kaplowitz believe assessing the library's instructional program can lead to the advancement of the program and its position with the institution. They write, 'Assessments can be used to provide information on the effectiveness of new and existing ILI programs' (Kaplowitz and Grassian, 2009). Assessment results can be shown to administrators and budget committees and 'This is a way for the library to document its contributions to the institution, to the goals and mission of the parent organization, and the advancement of student learning' (Kaplowitz and Grassian, 2009). Choosing a method of assessment is just as important as choosing an instructional method. As a library begins making decisions on a method of instruction, it should also be choosing a way to measure its effectiveness and criteria for success.

# References

Algon, J. (1997) Classifications of Tasks, Steps, and Information-related Behaviours of Individuals on Project Teams. In Jannica Hiensrtom's dissertation 'Fast Surfers, Broad Scanners and Deep Divers: Personality and Information-seeking Behaviour.' Available at *http://participants.abo.fi/jheinstr/parmbild.pdf*.

Anderson, L.W. and Krathwohl, D.R. (Eds.). (2001) *A Taxonomy for Learning, Teaching, and Assessing: a Revision of Bloom's Taxonomy of Educational Objectives*. New York: Longman.

Association of College and Research Libraries. (2000) Information Literacy Competency Standards for Higher Education. Available at *http://www.ala.org/ala/mgrps/divs/acrl/standards/informationliteracycompetency.cfm*.

Bandura, A. (1997) *Self-efficacy: The Exercise of Control*. New York: W.H. Freeman.

Battle, J. (2004) The Effect of Information Literacy Instruction on Library Anxiety among International Students. Doctoral dissertation, U of North Texas, May, 2004. Proquest Information and Learning Company, 3126554.

Beile, J. and Boote, D. (2005) Does the Medium Matter?: A Comparison of a Web-based Tutorial with Face-to-Face Library Instruction on Education Students' Self-efficacy Levels and Learning Outcomes. *Research Strategies*, 20: 57–68.

Cassidy, S. and Eachus, P. (1998) Developing the Computer Self-efficacy (CSE) Scale: Investigating the Relationship

Between CSE, Gender and Experience with Computers. *Journal of Educational Computing Research*, 26(2): 133–53.

Grassian, E. and Kaplowitz, J. (2009) *Information Literacy Instruction: Theory and Practice*. New York, NY: Neal-Schuman.

Hiensrtom, J. (2002) Dissertation. Fastsurfers, Broad Scanners and Deep Divers; Personality and Information-Seeking Behavior. Available at *http://participants.abo.fi/ jheinstr/parmbild.pdf*.

Hotchkiss, P. (2007) Personal interview at Cochise College Library with Director of Libraries.

Hotchkiss, P. (2009) Personal interview at Cochise College Library with Director of Libraries.

Jiao, Q.G. and Onwuegbuzie, A.J. (1997) Antecedents of Library Anxiety. *Library Quarterly*, 67(4): 372–89.

Jiao, Q.G. and Onwuegbuzie, A.J. (1999) Self-perception and Library Anxiety: An Empirical Study. *Library Review*, 48(3): 140–7.

Keene, J., Colvin, J. and Sissons, J. (2010) Mapping Student Information Literacy Activity against Bloom's Taxonomy of Cognitive Skills. *Journal of Information Literacy*, 4(1): 6–20. Available at *http://ojs.lboro.ac.uk/ojs/index.php/JIL/ article/view/PRA-V4-I1–2010–1*.

Krikelas, J. (1983) Information Seeking Behavior: Patterns and Concepts. *Drexel Library Quarterly*, 19(2): 5–20.

Kurbanoglu, S. (2009) Self-efficacy: An Alternative Approach to the Evaluation of Information Literacy. *Available at http:// www.isast.org/proceedingsQQML2009/PAPERS_PDF/ Kurbanoglu-Self_Efficacy_An_Alternative_Approach_to_ the_Evaluation_of_IL_PAPER-QQML 2009.pdf*.

Limberg, L. (1997) Information Use for Learning Purposes. In Jannica Hiensrtom's dissertation 'Fast Surfers, Broad

Scanners and Deep Divers Personality and Information-seeking Behaviour.' Available at *http://participants.abo.fi/ jheinstr/parmbild.pdf*.

Martin, B.L. (1989) A Checklist for Designing Instruction in the Affective Domain. *Educational Technology*, 29(8): 7–15.

Mellon, C.A. (1986). Library Anxiety: A Grounded Theory and Its Development. *College and IResearch Libraries*. Vol. 47: pp. 160–5.

Mueller, J. (2010) Information Literacy Assessment, Available Online. North Central University. Available at *http:// jonathan.mueller.faculty.noctrl.edu/infolit assessments.htm*.

Nahl-Jakobovits, D. and Jakobovits, L.A. (1993) Bibliographic Instructional Design for Information Literacy: Integrating Affective and Cognitive Objectives. *Research Strategies*, 11: 73–88.

National Postsecondary Education Cooperative (NPEC). (2005) NPEC Sourcebook on Assessment: Definitions and Assessment Methods for Communication, Leadership, Information Literacy, Quantitative Reasoning, and Quantitative Skills. Available at *http://nces.ed.gov/ pubs2005/2005832.pdf*.

North Central Association of Colleges and Schools. The Higher Learning Commission. (2003) *Handbook of Accreditation* (2nd ed). Available at *http://www .ncahigherlearningcommission.org*.

Northern Illinois University Office of Assessment Services. (2010) A History of Assessment. Available at *http://www .niu.edu/assessment/Manual/history.shtml*.

Onwuegbuzie, J., Jiao, Q. and Bostick, S. (2004) *Library Anxiety: Theory, Research, and Applications*. Lanham, MD: Scarecrow Press.

Radcliff, C., Jensen, M., Salem, A., Burhanna, K. and Gedeon, J. (2007) *A Practical Guide to Information*

*Literacy Assessment for Academic Librarians*. Westport, CT: Libraries Unlimited Publishing.

Ren, W. (2000) Library Instruction and College Student Self-efficacy in Electronic Information Searching. *The Journal of Academic Librarianship*, 26(5): 323–8.

Samson, S. (2010) Information Literacy Learning Outcomes and Student Success. *The Journal of Academic Librarianship*, 36(3): 202–10.

Saunders, L. (2007) Regional Accreditation Organizations' Treatment of Information Literacy: Definitions, Outcomes, and Assessment. *The Journal of Academic Librarianship*, 33(3): 317–26.

Schroeder, R. and Cahoy, E. (2010) Valuing information literacy: affective learning and the ACRL standards. *Portal: Libraries and the Academy*, 10(2): 127–46.

Simmonds, P.L. and Andaleeb, S.S. (2001) Usage of academic libraries: The role of service quality, resources, and participant characteristics. *Library Trends*, 49(4): 626–34.

Trombley, W. (2003, Winter) The rising price of higher education. College affordability. Available at *http://www.highereducation.org/reports/affordability_supplement/*.

Waldman, M. (2003) Freshmen's Use of Library Electronic Resources and Self-efficacy. *Information Research*, 8(2), paper no. 150. Available at *http://informationr.net/ir/8-2/paper150.html*.

# 3

# Participant populations, library environments, and learning environments

**Abstract:** This chapter describes the characteristics of participant groups, library environments, and learning environments. Though most of this book focuses on the academic library, this chapter includes descriptions of all library environments and the different learning environments used for instruction. It is said that a library is a library is a library; however, library participants come in all shapes and sizes, from the very young to senior citizens, and are as diverse in abilities and culture as they are in age. Accommodating such diversity is challenging and makes choosing an effective method of instruction all the more imperative for library instructional programs. The chapter will define types of participants including educational and skill levels. The library environments are categorized into public, academic (including school), and special. The learning environments are limited to face-to-face and virtual. Knowing your participants and environment is an essential factor and should not be overlooked when building the equation for choosing an effective method of instruction.

**Key words:** Library participants, library participant diversity, library users, multiculturalism, ethnicity, library environments, school libraries, academic libraries, public libraries, special libraries, virtual library instruction, online library instruction, face-to-face library instruction, online library tutorials.

## Participants

Knowing the participants who receive the instruction is equally as important as choosing an instructional method and an effectiveness measure. Grassian and Kaplowitz consider this a foundational element when developing an instructional program. They write 'Who are your learners? This is one of the most fundamental questions when developing an ILI program' (Grassian and Kaplowitz, 2009). There are many issues to consider when determining library participants, including gender, race/ethnicity, sexual orientation, socioeconomic status, religion, age, language, and ability and skill levels. This section addresses some of these issues and presents some assessment ideas on how to identify participant groups before selecting an instructional method.

### *Types of participants*

Library participant populations reflect the community where the library is located. Public library participants are made up from the neighborhood around the library and can be limited in cultural differences but be diverse in age and abilities. The limited cultural aspect can be true of school libraries also. Academic libraries and special libraries are not restricted by community constraints and tend to include diversity across all library participant characteristics. Some of the most common characteristics that affect a librarian's choice in mode of instruction are age, gender, ethnicity, multiculturalism and abilities.

#### Age, the non-traditional student

According to the US Department of Education, the number of non-traditional or adult learners has been steadily increasing since 1990 and will increase another 33 percent over the next five years (Department of Education, 2010). Non-traditional learners include youth and adults who do not come to college directly from high school, as well as underrepresented groups. Underrepresented groups include Native Americans, women and youth at risk, and adults on social assistance. They are also known as re-entry learners. This increasing population of older learners presents many different instructional challenges and levels of anxiety. They also have a widely varied educational background, familiarity with technology and acceptance of technology (Grassian and Kaplowitz, 2009). These learners can range from highly educated individuals with extensive technological experience to undereducated individuals who have never turned on a computer. It is vital to identify the strengths and weaknesses of the students before instruction begins.

Their approach to learning also varies from that of a traditional or youth learner, and educational experts have recommended a different learning paradigm called andragogy. Malcolm Knowles, a well-known American adult educator, developed andragogy theory in an attempt to specifically address adult learning. His theory emphasized that adult learners are self-directed and feel responsible for their own decisions. Knowles' theory assumed adult learners needed to know why they were learning something, they approached learning as problem solving, and they needed to see an immediate value in the instruction (Knowles, 1984(1)). Andragogy is based on the following principles:

1. Adults need to be involved in the planning and evaluation of their instruction.
2. Experience (including mistakes) provides the basis for learning activities.

3. Adults are most interested in learning subjects that have immediate relevance to their job or personal life.
4. Adult learning is problem-centered rather than content-oriented.

Librarians need to remember certain requirements when applying these principles to ILI. First, adult learners need the instructor to explain why specific things are being taught, for example why information literacy is important to them, and how their learning to find and evaluate information will be beneficial. Next the instructor must make the instruction task-oriented instead of a matter of memorization – learning activities should be in the context of common tasks to be performed. The librarian should involve the students in active learning exercises. If in a face-to-face class, the instruction should take place in a computer lab so the students can perform searches and learn how to use the databases as the instruction takes place. Additionally, the instruction should take into account the wide range of backgrounds of learners; learning materials and activities should allow for different levels/types of previous experience with computers. The instruction could begin with a refresher lesson on website access and navigation before getting into more advanced searching strategies. Finally, since adults are self-directed, instruction should allow learners to discover things for themselves, providing guidance and help when mistakes are made. The librarian should be the 'guide on the side' instead of the 'sage on the stage,' acting more as a facilitator than as an authoritative expert on the subject (Grassian and Kaplowitz, 2009).

Non-traditional learners require a learner-centered approach when designing an instructional method. They have a better idea of what is useful to them from instruction and want to be involved in their learning. They require an atmosphere of mutuality where they feel they are considered teachers as well as students in the instruction (Grassian and Kaplowitz, 2009). The instruction should be designed in a series of face-to-face and online workshops that the students can attend in order, or pick and choose from, depending on their skills and abilities. Librarians at the University of Denver, Penrose Library developed a set of workshops for LIS students using andragogy concepts to help the students develop library and information literacy skills. Figure 3.1 lists the learning objectives of the workshops they developed

**Figure 3.1** Learning objectives of adult learners' workshops

1A. *Beginner's technology*

Learning objectives: understand the basic functions of computer and Internet navigation, become familiar with the computer hardware and use of computer hardware.

1B. *Library services, collections and resources*

Learning objectives: understand how library materials are organized, become familiar with library services and resources, and explore the library web portal.

2. *Searching peak: The library catalog*

Learning objectives: use the library OPAC to locate books, reference materials, e-books, government documents, maps, and print periodicals; locate and request materials in Prospector; and request an interlibrary loan.

3. *Basic research strategies*

Learning objectives: understand the concepts, techniques, and tools for creating an effective search strategy, and become familiar with typical research assignments.

4. *Databases for librarians*

Learning objectives: become familiar with specific research databases, conduct keyword and subject searches, locate and assess results, and refine searches using basic database features.

5. *Advanced database skills*

Learning objectives: use advanced search options, understand how to use the built-in database features (thesaurus, subject guide, index, journal list, and more).

(*Continued*)

**Figure 3.1** Learning objectives of adult learners' workshops *(cont'd)*

> 6. *Internet resources for librarians*
>    Learning objectives: become familiar with free Internet reference resources, including tutorials, pathfinders, resource guides, open access databases, academic and government resources, and virtual directories created for librarians and information specialists.
> 7. *Evaluating Internet resources*
>    Learning objectives: understand some basic techniques for evaluating and validating Internet resources.
> 8. *Academic writing skills in the APA style*
>    Learning objectives: to become familiar with the basics of the writing style of the American Psychological Association (APA), and most particularly how to use the APA Publication Manual to appropriately write papers and cite sources.
>
> **Plan outline for Session 3: Basic research strategies**
>
> *First provide students with any relevant handouts, for example if there is powerpoint presentation, the slides in a handout form, or a page of links to the resources used in the demonstration.*
>
> Overview of the need for these workshops
>
> State objectives and review roadmap
>
> Article critiques
>
> Effective searching and searching objectives
>
> Discussion/definition of databases
>
> Active learning: assignment – define peer-reviewed/scholarly journals
>
> Searching for an appropriate scholarly article using the Penrose website
>
> Step-by-step instructions for getting into a database in the Penrose website, and explanation of the screens
>
> Using LISTA database with basic search and advanced search
>
> Evaluating and locating an article
>
> Closure: Review objectives, discuss Pathfinder, answer questions, and request completion of evaluation

*Source*: Goldman, Hunter and Shelton (2007)

with an additional beginner's technology workshop and a copy of the single lesson plan for one of the workshops. Each lesson plan incorporates an active learning component to involve the student in the instruction (Goldman, Hunter and

Shelton, 2007). The population of adult learners will continue to increase in the next decade and will make up a considerable percentage of students receiving ILI. Librarians should consider developing appropriate self-pace face-to-face and online tutorials to accommodate them.

## Gender

Research has shown females and males learn differently. The results of the studies vary widely and numerous basic differences have been presented. Women tend to have better verbal skills and adjust better to educational structure. Additionally, studies indicate women are more connected learners (Grassian and Kaplowitz, 2009) and prefer a more learner centered instructional method. In contrast, men are more separate learners and prefer the teacher-centered method of instruction (Grassian and Kaplowitz, 2009). The US Department of Education maintains statistics on academic performance and, according to its records, girls are approximately one and a half years ahead of boys in reading and writing competency. Boys are two to four points higher than girls in math and science test scores (US Department of Education, 2010). Girls receive about 60 percent of the As across all levels of education and boys receive 70 percent of the Ds and Fs. Over the past two decades, researchers have documented that males have distinct technological skills advantages over females (Wever-Rabehl, 2006). Educational research has shown that many of these gender advantages and disadvantages are due to a gender bias by teachers within the educational systems. Michael Gurian, a renowned expert in brain research, believes the differences are brain-based. He presents neurological evidence that male and female brain structure is the direct causal factor for these gender learning differences. He also claims the learning differences are not due to bias-based teaching and believes that teachers lack the adequate information they require to teach males and females (Gurian et al., 2001). Gurian's research used brain scans to show male and female brains try to learn the same things in very different ways and teachers need to be trained in how the brain learns in males and females. This strategy is called nature-based teaching and is an approach that involves creating a learning environment conducive to both genders' brain systems. A nature-based approach is a long-term strategy and would not apply to most information literacy instructional methods; however, it is beneficial for librarians to be aware of gender learning differences.

## Ethnicity and multiculturalism

By the year 2020, one out of every three Americans will be a person of color, and students of color will make up almost 50 percent of the student population. In the lifetimes of many of today's college and university students, non-Hispanic whites are predicted to become less than half the population of the United States (Meacham, 2003). In the twenty-first century, diversity is a word with a high degree of elasticity and has expanded far beyond minority racial groups. The term can include race and ethnicity, and define persons with physical or mental disabilities, or address a person's sexual orientation. Most libraries have recognized the importance of addressing the issue of multiculturalism and diversity, and developed policies demonstrating a commitment to equality for all participants. It is important for librarians to become aware of the instructional difficulties that exist and are unique to each group of participants. Anne Switzer, an outreach librarian at Oakland University, believes there are different obstructions that apply to each group of participants. She writes, 'Attention is finally beginning to be placed on other "nontraditional" users – that is, any student who differs from the typical college student with regard to abilities, age, gender/sexuality, nationality or ethnicity, and locale (students taking classes at a remote campus and/or online). The educational barriers are different for each separate population; they are, nonetheless, significant enough to warrant our consideration' (Switzer, 2008). The library environment is fast-changing and librarians can be leaders in the information literacy education of non-traditional groups of participants.

A common instructional obstacle with a diverse population of participants is language. Many of these non-traditional learners are also learning English and only speak English when in an educational environment. Grassian and Kaplowitz write, 'Many of these users speak their native language at home and in their communities and must switch to English for their educational experiences' (Grassian and Kaplowitz, 2009). English-language learners are trying to study in a language different from their own and in most cases are trying to acclimate to a new culture. Librarians must expand their efforts in making these students feel welcome and comfortable. A hands-on, active learning approach works well with these students, keeping the instructions direct and defining all library jargon in easy-to-understand language. Always try to have the students apply the instruction and perform tasks to obtain immediate feedback. This will provide a performance assessment of how well the participants have retained what was being taught. Grassian and Kaplowitz recommend employing numerous instructional strategies to help with training and educating this group of users: 'Gestures, graphic illustrations, handouts, rephrasing, speaking slowly and clearly and restating ideas are all methods that can help these learners' (Grassian and Kaplowitz, 2009). These learners will work better at their own pace and should be allowed to interact with the instructional materials instead of sitting through a lecture presentation. Online tutorials for repeated viewings and web-based guides in multiple languages are also beneficial in helping these learners develop library and informational skills (Grassian and Kaplowitz, 2009).

Another group of learners brought to the forefront as education has raised the priority on diversity are people with physical and/or mental disabilities. The Americans with Disabilities Act (ADA) raised awareness of disabled people and brought about policies to accommodate this group of learners. In education, the trend has shifted to integrating disabled learners into regular programs instead of providing special programming for them (Grassian and Kaplowitz, 2009). Librarians are encountering this group of participants more often and must consider the special techniques required in their education. Disabled does not mean these participants are dependent or helpless; they usually lead lives just like those of people who are not disabled and their disability is often separate from matters of cognition. When in doubt as to what special assistance is required for a disabled student, simply ask him or her and be flexible to meeting their needs. Another segment of the disabled population vulnerable to not receiving the library services are the deaf. Deaf students can require extensive instruction in library skills since many hearing-impaired students have lower levels of knowledge in the area (Mason, 2010). Few librarians have acquired the skills necessary to meet the needs of the deaf student, and improvements are needed in this area. A good strategy for elevating the ILI experience for the deaf is to maintain a good collaborative relationship with the disabled services unit who can provide sign translators for instructional sessions. The library should design instruction that is all-inclusive, and this includes addressing Lesbian/Gay/Bisexual/Transexual students. Instruction can include pathfinders to resources that challenge the silence about LGBT issues. In this way, librarians can be leaders in diminishing homophobia, contributing to a tolerant and healthy learning environment for everyone. A library serves a population that is ever growing in numbers and diversity; as librarians we need to make our services available to all. The best way to attain this goal is to talk with members of all participant groups to identify the best possible ways to include them and their needs in the design of instruction.

## Abilities

Abilities of participants can be as diverse as the participant population and include deficiencies in everything from academic skills to technology literacy. Educational backgrounds vary among participants and many lack the skill sets needed to navigate the complexities of the information available in the twenty-first century library. These participants require patience and flexibility in instruction. It may be important to limit the amounts of information presented in the instructional period, and the librarian should try to involve students in learning activities instead of expecting the participants to sit through continuous lecture. It is important to recognize that participants are going to possess different levels of academic and cognitive abilities and adjust the instructional method as you go. Participants with limited skill sets tend to fall through the cracks at most educational levels and go unnoticed. In addition to adjusting instruction, librarians can offer walk-in and by-appointment help, also encouraging these participants to enroll in writing skills classes offered at writing labs.

All the above mentioned participants usually have some level of problem with the library classification system, underdeveloped critical thinking skills, variations in educational backgrounds, and technological difficulties. These problems can be amplified by cultural differences in learning styles, and librarians should be urged to 'become proficient at cultural appraisal and more sensitive to cultural differences' (Switzer, 2008). It is also important to know the composition of the overall participant population and become familiar with the traits and needs of all participants. The best strategy is to vary and combine the instructional methods in an attempt to reach all the learners (Grassian and Kaplowitz, 2009).

## Library environments

This publication's main focus is academic libraries. However, in the pursuit of promoting life-long learning, the foundational building block of information literacy instruction, it is appropriate to mention all library environments. There are three main types of libraries, public, academic, and special. Though ILI has mainly been associated with academic libraries, the widespread movement of information literacy has brought the importance of teaching IL skills to the forefront in all environments. Each type of library serves a different population of participants, but all participants have the same basic need; they are looking for information. The current world of information is vast and continues to expand daily. As the quantity of information grows, the skills needed to find reliable, accurate information also increase. Libraries have been providing this epistemological service for centuries and are the ideal organizations to teach others the skills required to navigate the overwhelming amounts of information now available. The world is changing with technological advances and in the future subsistence will require a certain level of information literacy skills. Teaching these skills is now needed in every library to expose all participants to the skills they will need. This section will outline the different types of libraries and some of the instructional problems each type encounters.

## Public libraries

For most people, this is what is considered a library: a public building that provides books and reference and is mainly used by senior citizens and children. Public libraries are everywhere and are considered fundamental in promoting a literate population. The locations vary as much as the diversity in the participants. Instructional classes of the public library usually focus on direct self-help needs of the community, ranging from basic literacy skills to US citizenship information. Many participants only have computer access through their public libraries; consequently the public library has become a provider of computer-skills instruction. These assorted instructional opportunities are conducted in various ways, face-to-face class offerings, one-on-one point of use instruction with a single participant, and online tutorials.

Though the gap is narrowing, there are still a large number of participants on the wrong side of the digital divide. As it becomes more necessary for people to have access to and skills in computer technology, the role of the public library in these participants' education will become more challenging. Many of these participants have never used a computer and require extensive instruction before being able to do an Internet search. Compounding this influx of digital dividers is the increasing use of the library by K-12 students. Because of the recent economic crunch, many schools have been forced to discontinue support, leaving the students to use the public library for their information needs (Grassian and

Kaplowitz, 2009). This has created a demand that puts a strain on an already overworked public library staff. The average public librarian has never acquired the teaching experience to provide the instructional services called for by this increasing population of participants who need to acquire information literacy skills. As with any institution that relies on public sources for its finances, public libraries are facing budgetary challenges. An increasing demand for computer access puts even greater pressure on decreasing budgets and has public libraries scrambling for additional sources of income (Grassian and Kaplowitz, 2009). Marketing of librarianship and the occupation may increase the number of librarians. Once these librarians are in an MLS program the institutions must increase the credit hours spent on preparing librarians for instruction. Organizational classes and Foundations are all well and good; however, most of a librarian's time is now spent in one-on-one or full class instruction and should be considered the greatest educational need of a library science student. As stated by Grassian and Kaplowitz, 'Funding, of course, is always an issue.' One possible solution is to recruit community agencies and private businesses in addressing the participants' instructional needs. An informed and information literate public can only enrich the community and should be an incentive for cooperation.

## *Academic libraries*

Academic libraries cover a far-ranging spectrum, from libraries in all types of schools to the libraries at major universities. Most consider secondary education school libraries as a separate class of library; however, these libraries serve students and should be considered academic libraries. Diversity in participant population is as great as that of the public library, though most participants share one common

## Participant populations, library environments, learning environments

characteristic: they are all students. The population also consists of the teachers and faculty of the parent institution. The role of the academic library is to provide access to information and services that support student learning. There is a long history of instruction in academic libraries and their popularity has increased with the growth of the information literacy movement in recent years. The demand for critical thinking skills has also increased recently. As this demand has expanded, students have been encouraged to expand their informational horizons. Another popular movement within educational environments is the focus on distance learning at every level of education. All these recent developments in education have created more opportunities for ILI than ever before.

Accountability has become an issue for all academic libraries. K-12 to higher education institutions are being pressured to deliver a better product. Secondary schools are being criticized by higher education institutions for advancing students who are not prepared for college-level work. Employers and businesses are complaining that the students from higher education institutions do not have the skills needed to compete in today's globalized society. The institutions are demanding that the libraries shoulder more responsibility and contribute more to student learning. Meeting these demands is made even more difficult when the librarians are faced with uncooperative faculty. Producing evidence that ILI is effective in increasing student learning takes a great effort in collaboration between the faculty and the librarians. Though some institutions enjoy a collaborative relationship between instructors and librarians, many libraries are faced with a tough challenge of convincing the faculty to integrate IL into their curriculums. At a time when the library is being asked to increase its participation in student learning, many institutions are cutting libraries' budgets. Another issue is the complexity of timing and scheduling of ILI sessions (Grassian and Kaplowitz, 2009). Getting faculty to give up class time to accommodate a library instructional session is another challenge in the librarian/instructor collaboration relationship. The best way to attack this set of problems is with a well laid out strategic plan for ILI. To start, librarians need to establish solid relationships with the faculty. Use every opportunity to interact with faculty – faculty orientations, special faculty convocations, meet-and-greets at the library inviting the faculty members. Involve the faculty in collection development, get their opinions on resources the library should be acquiring that target their classes and curriculums. Any positive contact will go a long way in developing the collaboration needed for a fully integrated IL program in the process of student learning. If the library wants to continue playing a vital role in the infrastructure of academics it must show how it supports student learning. Integrating the ILI program into class curriculums ties the library directly to the learning process and gives the library the opportunity to increase student learning.

## *Special libraries*

Any library that is not a public library or an academic library could be considered a special library. Special libraries serve a single institution and tend to be a single-subject library. These libraries are designed to support the mission of the organization and their collections are focused on resources that target the specific needs of the employees who work there. Special libraries include law libraries, news libraries, government libraries, corporate libraries, museum libraries, and medical libraries. These libraries specialize in serving the organization and do not allow access to the public. Many special library collections are made up solely of internal documents including annual reports, financial statements, project descriptions and memos. Everyone who works for the organization has access to the library, from the administration to the maintenance employees. Librarians in special libraries are more specialist in information about the organization than they are librarians, and many are referred to as information officer or information scientist rather than librarian.

The role of the special library is tied to the organization's bottom line and profits, not to the advancement of an information literate public, nor the education of students. Consequently, their position is under constant pressure to justify the existence of the library. Information literacy instruction plays a minor role in the structure of the special library, mostly designed to inform employees on the use of new resources and the online catalog if one is available. The librarian must learn as much as possible about the information the organization uses and learn the needs of employees. Executing a push strategy is beneficial and librarians have to develop an intuitive characteristic of what information will be needed at certain times. Many organizations are cyclical and this becomes routine. An important element is proving the library's value to the organization and this is done by delivering the right information at the right times.

## Learning environments

ILI can be presented in many different ways: stand-alone courses, course-integrated sessions, general one-shot orientations, the drop-in or drive-by bibliographic instruction, point-of-use guides, pathfinders and web-based module tutorials. Delivery methods or learning environments are much more limited. The material can be delivered face-to-face in a regular classroom setting or electronically through computerization. Technology has blurred these lines recently with the introduction of video-conferencing software such as Elluminate Live, which allows librarians to teach a class over the Internet in real time to distance learners anywhere, anytime. This section will describe the two learning environments and some of the advantages and disadvantages of using them.

## Face-to-face

Face-to-face (FTF) learning groups are the traditional method of education everywhere. The instructor delivers content to a class of students while physically located in the same room with the students. Many students, regardless of generation, prefer this environment, stating it gives them structure and routine. It provides them with access to the instructor that just is not there in an online environment. There have been countless studies comparing face-to-face with online learning with mixed results. Recently, more studies show there is no difference between the learning environment and the learning outcomes of students. The differences are now often measured in the perception of the advantages and disadvantages. The face-to-face environment offers numerous advantages to the student:

1. *Process familiarity.* Live learning is what most of us are familiar with and have grown up experiencing (Faust, 2000). Many students feel more comfortable and experience less library anxiety when in a group of familiar peers.

2. *Connectedness.* Being with other students, asking questions and getting immediate feedback creates a feeling of connectedness, of being part of a real class.

Two-way communication allows establishment of rapport between instructor and student (Faust, 2000). The students get to see and relate to the librarian, and the librarian has an opportunity to develop a relationship with the students.

3. *Student response.* Instructors can easily and immediately identify student response to material and can respond instantly if students seem confused or puzzled by material (Faust, 2000). Responding to students' confusion shows a sense of caring from the librarian.

4. *Feedback.* Student questions receive immediate response; these is no waiting period during which the student may forget the question or misunderstand the response (Faust, 2000). A response to an e-mail that may be hours or even days old seems less meaningful.

5. *Closer relationship.* Face-to-face instruction always develops a closer relationship between the student and librarian, and the student is more apt to approach a librarian after attending a face-to-face instructional session.

6. *Clear and full communication.* Learners and librarian communicate with each other in back-and-forth verbal communication – a more common and direct way with less misunderstanding of content.

7. *Easy to monitor.* Librarians can monitor how the students are interpreting the instruction; the learning and content presentation can all be monitored and altered if needed, depending on the pace of student learning and skill level.

Some of the disadvantages of face-to-face learning environments are that the learners have to attend scheduled sessions at a specific time and place. For today's participants this can be difficult and inconvenient. Also, learners with

English as a second language can struggle with understanding the content, and require additional assistance from the librarian. In an online environment, the content could be translated with web-based translation software if needed. Unlike distance-learning classes, ILI-online tutorial modules are more cost effective than face-to-face library instruction. The initial expense is offset by the number of students that can continue to access the set of modules numerous times without any extra expense. Perhaps the greatest disadvantage of face-to-face classes is on the librarian-side of the instruction. The development and delivery time of face-to-face ILI has created a whole new occupation and made the librarian into the teacher. More time is spent on instruction now than on the traditional tasks of the librarian. Measuring the utility of this is difficult. Comparatively, the instruction is bringing a job-security aspect to the position, though it does distract from other responsibilities of the librarian, especially in the smaller libraries where the librarian wears many hats and the job description expands to include numerous duties. The majority of students overlook the disadvantages of FTF instruction and that is why the one-shot library instructional period is still the most popular presentation method for ILI (Grassian and Kaplowitz, 2009).

As stated above, there are numerous modes of ILI presentation. There are the stand-alone courses that involve a full semester credit-bearing class with a full curriculum. These are usually offered as 100 level for undergraduates and 500 level for graduate students. Another method is course-integrated sessions, where through collaboration with a faculty member, the librarian designs a single session that targets a specific class assignment. These are also called just-in-time sessions, sometimes scheduled just before the assignment is due. There are also general one-shot orientations, the most popular ILI design. These are usually one-class-period sessions that present the resources the library holds and teach the students how to find and use resources to help them in a particular discipline. Finally, there is the drop-in or drive-by bibliographic instruction. These are short 10–15 minute instructional sessions that introduce the librarians and some of the services the library offers to the students. The last two designs have been used as marketing tools. The popularity of distance learning is increasing the use of electronic instruction, but FTF instruction is still likely the preferred learning environment of most students.

## *Electronic*

Electronic ILI is usually web based and participants can access it anytime from anywhere that provides Internet access. The instruction is often presented in learning modules that direct a student through the research cycle, from developing keywords to using the library's databases and concluding with lessons on the correct use of information to avoid plagiarism. Many online tutorials include interactivity and encourage the participant to actively participate in the instruction, providing tests with immediate feedback and appealing interfaces. There are three main types of interactive learning systems used in library online tutorials: drill-and-practice, tutorials, and simulations (Tancheva, 2003). Drill-and-practice systems are designed to reinforce skills a participant already possesses. The participant has already learned the content in previous lessons and is using the instruction to refresh or advance their knowledge of it. In contrast, tutorials teach a participant new material and use evaluative tools to verify that the participant has understood the instruction. Simulations replicate the experience of a task and employ graphics and visualization techniques. These types of tutorial systems can use complex illustrations created with Flash software to enhance the learning experience of the participant.

Another popular tool being used to create online tutorials is screencasting software. This allows a librarian to capture the activity taking place on a computer screen, create a running video from the screen captures and embed audio content into the video. Another new form of tutorial ILI presentation has been short videos. The videos are usually 2–3 minute presentations that cover a range of topics from general (e.g. evaluating websites and using wikipedia) to how to navigate specific databases to using different library services (e.g. interlibrary loan). Many academic libraries employ students as the actors, with background music and special effects added. Libraries provide a link on their web page to the screencast or video, and participants can just click and the instruction is streamed to their computer. There has been some limited experimentation with developing a gaming version of ILI. Some academic libraries have integrated gaming strategies into their ILI. Games are a large portion of the popular culture and libraries view them as an effective way to attract young participants to using their online ILI. Finally, video conferencing software is another new technology in the electronic environment. It is a way to bring the face-to-face experience into the electronic environment. This tool allows the librarian to perform live ILI sessions delivered over the Internet to anyone with computer access. Elluminate Live video conferencing software is being used in many online learning environments, such as Blackboard, D2L, and Moodle, with great success. The shift to online instruction has already begun, and all libraries should investigate these new presentation methods and prepare to deliver a web-based ILI.

The electronic learning environment has many advantages, especially for the distance learner. Web-based ILI presents the same information to every participant and removes any variations of human delivery (Smith, 2001). Online ILI tutorials can be used at the participant's convenience, they can be accessed from anywhere, they offer an alternative to regular learning to self-motivated learners and are more beneficial to visual learners. Further, because of the multimedia features of the electronic environment, online ILI is considered more capable of satisfying the diversity in learning styles (Tancheva, 2001). Designing a multiple-module tutorial is more cost effective, especially when the instruction has to be presented to thousands of new incoming students. Possibly the most significant advantage of web-based ILI is the characteristic of the instruction being at the precise point of need for a participant. This is, of course, assuming the participant will go to the tutorial when they need help with their research (Tancheva, 2003). The disadvantages include less participant satisfaction; studies have shown that learners are less satisfied with content structure of online ILI compared with FTF and less satisfied with the interactivity both from the instruction and no-instructor interaction. Another complaint is that traditional content of ILI does not translate well into the electronic environment and unless the library's mission and infrastructure are geared towards web based ILI, online instruction can be inappropriate and difficult to implement (Smith, 2001). A further concern with online tutorials is that too often these tutorials are seen as using technology for its own sake (Mason, 2000) rather than for the enhancement of learning. All of these disadvantages are pratical, not theoretical (Tancheva, 2003), and through application and practice can be overcome. Distance learning is the way of the future and web-based ILI will become more ubiquitous as more participants access all forms of education and training online.

## Take-home message

No matter what the library or learning environment, the population of participants will be diverse, and knowing the participants is fundamental in determining what instructional method will be effective. As Grassian and Kaplowitz say, 'A library is a library is a library' (Grassian and Kaplowitz, 2009). However, this is not true of participants: they and their needs are as diverse as the world's population. There is no way of stereotyping your participant population. Though difficult, it is best to think of each participant as an individual requiring special treatment. Though ILI is currently limited in public libraries, they will start to include ILI as a regular service as more everyday subsistence requires Internet access. Watch for the public sector to start demanding more ILI sessions at their community libraries as more government services and information become web based. Public participants are already asking for regular computer skills instruction as the Internet becomes a greater influence in their lives. A long-held misconception is that academic libraries have somewhat of a captive audience in the academic community. The organization they serve exists to teach and its participants are there to learn, and the libraries' role in all this is to provide information that supports teaching and learning. This does not detract from the challenges of providing an effective ILI program. Academic libraries and librarians are responsible for a high level of accountability and are in a constant struggle to justify that their services contribute to student learning. Developing an effective ILI program in this competitive environment requires a great deal of collaboration with the faculty to show the library's contribution to student learning. Special libraries must always prove their value to their organization's bottom line and show how their services are contributing to profits. Special librarians, more than their counterparts in public and academic libraries, must learn to be intuitive to the employees' and administrators' needs and promote the information that fulfills those needs. All library environments are in a battle with competing entities for funding and usually lose in the budget-cut war. There have been so many contrasting results in studies measuring differences between FTF and electronic learning environment that it is hard to determine whether any differences exist or not. As the next chapter will show, there is one preferred environment; however, both have advantages and disadvantages to consider when choosing an effective ILI method. FTF offers the connectedness that creates a comfortable learning experience for participants. Electronic environments deliver the convenience multi-tasking participants are looking for in this modern society that often has to micromanage their time. A participant population with global diversity, different institutional environments, and learning environments makes choosing an effective ILI challenging and difficult in a time of escalating demands for IL.

# References

Department of Education. (2010) Fast Facts. National Center for Educational Statistics. Available at *http://nces.ed.gov/fastfacts/display.asp?id=98*.

Faust, J. (2000) Advantages of Face to Face Learning. Available at *http://stewardess.inhatc.ac.kr/philoint/teaching-data/Face-to-face-learning-vs.-Online-learning.htm*.

Goldman, S., Hunter, L. and Shelton, N. (2007) Roadmap to Library Resource and Research Skills. Available at *https://portfolio.du.edu/portfolio/getportfoliofile?uid*.

Grassian, E. and Kaplowitz, J. (2009) *Information Literacy Instruction: Theory and Practice*. New York, NY: Neal-Schuman.

Gurian, M., Henley, P. and Trueman, T. (2001) *Boys and Girls Learn Differently: A Guide for Parents and Teachers*. San Fransisco, CA: Jossey-Bass Publishing.

Knowles, M. (1984(1)) *The Adult Learner: A Neglected Species* (3rd ed.). Houston, TX: Gulf Publishing.

Knowles, M. (1984) *Andragogy in Action*. San Francisco: Jossey-Bass.

Mason, M. (2010) User Groups in Academic Libraries. MKM Research. Available at *http://www.moyak.com/papers/library-reference-service-users.html*.

Mason, R. (2000) From Distance Education to Online Education. *Internet and Higher Education*, 3 (1/2): 63–74.

Meacham, J., McClellan, M., Pearse, T. and Greene, R. (2003) Student Diversity in Classes and Educational Outcomes: Student Perceptions. *College Student Journal*. Available at *http://findarticles.com/p/articles/mi_m0FCR/is_4_37/ai_112720429/*.

Robles, R.C., Wang, P., Guion, J. and Heo, Y. (2007) Advantages of Online Learning. Available at *http://stewardess.inhatc.ac.kr/philoint/teaching-data/Face-to-face-learning-vs.-Online-learning.htm*.

Smith, Susan Sharpless. (2001) *Web-Based Instruction: A Guide for Libraries*. Chicago: ALA.

Switzer, Anne T. (2008) Redefining Diversity: Creating an Inclusive Academic Library through Diversity Initiatives. *College and Undergraduate Libraries*, 15: 3: 280–300.

Tancheva, K. (2003) Online Tutorials for Library Instruction: An Ongoing Project Under Constant Revision. Available at *http://www.ala.org/ala/mgrps/divs/acrl/events/pdf/tancheva.PDF*.

Wever-Rabehl, G. (2006) Gender and Education, A Gender Gap in Technology. Available at *http://www.suite101.com/content/wiredwomenspidermanandgender-a1831*.

# 4

# Effective ILI methods

**Abstract:** This chapter will focus on choosing an effective ILI method by presenting comparisons of the different methods mentioned in Chapter 2, traditional lecture instruction, active learning, computer assisted, learner centered and self directed. The chapter also presents evidence from a number of studies that show when one method is more effective over another method depending on the objective of the ILI program. Additionally, evidence is provided from several studies showing participants prefer the FTF method. There is also a section on how to select an effective method based on comparisons of methods. Considering all variables and making the best choice are challenging and hopefully this chapter reduces some of the anxiety of choosing an effective method for your population, environment and institution.

**Key words:** Information literacy instruction methods, effective library instruction, instructional goals, instructional objectives, traditional lecture instruction, active learning, computer-assisted instruction, learner-centered instruction, self-directed instruction, learning environments, face-to-face instruction, online tutorials.

## What to consider

As determined earlier, there is a plethora of topics, contact times, and delivery modes available when trying to determine which method of ILI to design for your institution. These elements can be blended in any number of ways, making a decision even more challenging. Then there are the tangible and intangible factors to consider, including inaudience, purpose (what is the objective of the program), cost, time, staff, equipment, software, facilities, materials, prep time, and the participants' availability. Additionally, impact factors need to be considered. What is the impact on other staff members? Will there be an extra workload for them as other staff work on the instruction? What will be the impact on the other programs within the library, the reference desk, circulation, technical services? Are there personal preferences to consider, the instructional staff, the administration's wants and needs, the participants themselves, and other faculty? (Grassian and Kaplowitz, 2009). All of this before you can consider the effectiveness of one method over another. The earlier chapters have listed variables that could be considered the most significant in an equation for designing an effective ILI. We have determined that there are five main methods of ILI, three measures of effectiveness (program objectives), participants, three library environments, and two learning environments. Grassian and Kaplowitz believe some of the most significant factors are the purpose of the program (objectives), the learning environment, and the participants. There are two common characteristics all participant populations share: diversity and the need for information. The diversity of participant populations makes choosing a single method based on your participants at best a difficult decision. One method will never be the best fit for all. So, let us first consider the single characteristic of need of information when basing your decision on participants. Since all participants are in need of information we will consider the most important factors when selecting to be program objective, teaching method, and learning environment. In the following sections we will assign methods of instruction based on objective, teaching method, and learning environment.

## Choosing based on objective

The environment has already been decided based on the institution that is choosing the method – whether it is public, academic, or special. Many institutions are not even in a position to choose a method because their situation chooses for them. For example, lack of staff or technology may impose limits. If they are in a position to choose, some basic groundwork should already have been completed before the selection process begins. Needs assessment will have identified your audience and the most important things they need to know – what knowledge will benefit them the most. Combining this with the institutional mission will be the foundation for the content of the instruction. If this is the first attempt the institution is making to choose an instructional method, a little research into other organizations' programs will also be beneficial. Conferences, workshops, and the web are all good sources of information for instructional content design. If the instruction will require any funds other than librarian time in the classroom, budget considerations should be determined. After all the preliminary work has been completed, it is time to choose, based on the most significant factor, the program objective – what the purpose of the instruction is. Do you want to change behavior? Do you want to make affective changes? Are you looking to make cognitive changes by increasing skills? This section will look at different program objectives and suggest effective methods for each effectiveness measure.

## Behavioral changes

As mentioned earlier, behavioral outcomes are changes in action (e.g. increased use of online library resources, use of librarians, use of the physical library itself, or a change in participant information seeking behavior). Changing an individual's behavior is done all the time in marketing. It consists of selling one's product or opinion and convincing others of the benefits of changing their behavior. To change behaviors one has to think like a marketer and develop a persuasive strategy. The Center for Social Marketing and Behavioral Change suggests almost the same strategy as we have here when choosing a method to change a behavior. They ask the following list of questions to decide what will be the most effective intervention to change an individual's behavior.

1. Who is the audience (identify participants)?
2. What do you want them to do (program objective)?
3. What influences the behavior (instructional content)?
4. What is most effective at changing the behavior (instructional method)? (Center for Social Marketing and Behavioral Change, 2010)

They create interventions in a variety of formats to change all types of social behaviors, including obesity and overeating, tobacco and drug use, and alcohol use. They use CD-ROMs, paper materials and face-to-face (FTF) lecturing. They use a combination of formats in different situations and believe their most effective method of persuasion is the use of the FTF lectures by a convincing expert in the field (Rangan, Karim and Sandberg, 2009).

There has been limited research measuring the effectiveness of ILI in increasing usage of a library. There are two studies

Effective ILI methods

that directly relate to affecting behavioral change using ILI. A 2004 study published in the *Journal of Academic Librarianship* by two researchers from a community college in the state of Washington measured the effectiveness of library instruction in increasing usage of the library by undergraduate students (Portmann and Roush, 2004). The purpose of the study was to ascertain the influence of one hour library instruction on undergraduate library usage and skills (i.e. does one hour of library instruction have a significant influence on library usage and skills?). The analysis indicated that library instruction delivered face to face in a one hour lecture significantly increased library usage while there was no significant increase in library skills. Another study performed by the author and presented at a lecture series at the School of Information Resources and Library Science of the University of Arizona measured the effect of two types of ILI on student library usage behavior. The purpose of this study was to determine whether ILI delivered in a one-hour traditional lecture method was effective in increasing students' usage of the physical library and the library's online resources. A second hypothesis of the study claimed that an active learning ILI delivered in two one-hour sessions would be more effective in increasing usage of the library and its online resources. The traditional lecture session used a curriculum similar to the one presented in Figure 1.1, and the active learning sessions used a curriculum similar to the one presented in Figure 1.2. The results of the study were mixed. The one-shot traditional lecture method was effective in increasing online usage and in-house usage; however, the in-house usage increase was not statistically significant. The two-session active learning method was significantly effective in increasing in-house use and online use of the library (Walsh, 2010). Marketing the library and its resources and trying to increase usage may be the most popular objective of ILI by all libraries. These examples show that FTF traditional lecture using a one-shot session is likely to be the most effective method for changing the behavior of participants. To change behavior requires persuasion and also some type of extrinsic or intrinsic reward. To effectively change the students' behavior, i.e. increase their usage of the library, the instruction needs to provide the information to the student on how they will be rewarded through use of the library. The content should focus on where to find resources, how to use them and how the usage of the resources will benefit the participants. If the library has the facilities and technology it would be advantageous to include an active learning element in the instruction. Involve the participants in the instruction by having them follow along and use the resources the librarian is presenting. As the following sections will show, active learning elements always significantly increase the effectiveness of the instruction, whatever measure is being used.

## Cognitive changes

Many academic libraries are defining their ILI program goals and objectives to increase participants' cognitive skills. This automatically ties the ILI program to student learning outcomes. If the program proves successful in increasing a participant's cognitive skills the library can use the evaluation results of the ILI program as accountability evidence and justify themselves and their services. Cognitive changes are changes in the knowledge of participants and relate to how people observe, think, problem solve, and remember (Grassian and Kaplowitz, 2009). The increases can be identified by library skills, such as identifying necessary information, extracting the required information, evaluating information critically, and using information from a wide range of resources. Additionally, increases can be indentified in actual student learning, including better grades on a standardized posttest and better grades in classes. Changing the cognitive skills of an individual is not as easy as persuading them to change their behavior. Many studies have shown that influencing participants' cognitive abilities is easier to do when the participant is required to think critically, rather than just informing the participant with information (Kohl and Wilson, 1986; Kunkel and Weaver, 1996; Madland and Hagness, 1998; Marcus and Beck, 2003; Small, Zakaria and El-Figuigui, 2004).

The Portmann and Roush study used a one-shot face-to-face ILI. They found it was not effective in increasing library skills and suggested it had no positive influence on student learning. Another study conducted by three librarian researchers at the University of California, Irvine, showed that one hour of ILI had no significant effect on students' GPAs, though a face-to-face for-credit class did. The study tested two groups of students over the duration of their college careers. One group was enrolled in an eight-week for-credit library course that taught IL skills in a face-to-face environment. The second group was not required to take any ILI and most received a one-shot face-to-face ILI session. On average, students who completed the library course were found to have 0.15-point higher GPAs and 2.9 more quarters of attendance than the control group (Selegean, Thomas and Richman, 1983). A similar study done by a Central Michigan University librarian measured the length of the impact of an eight-week for-credit face-to-face IL course. The study tested two groups of students: one group who had taken the class and one group not required to take the class who had one-shot ILI.

The researcher believed that the most interesting finding was the significantly increased paper grades and course final grades by the students who had taken the class over the students who had not. The increased paper and course grades were also recorded from one to two years after the students had taken the class. The researchers concluded that the length of instruction time and contact with the instructor were the influencing variables. Finally, a study conducted by librarian researchers at the University of New York, Oswego, found students who received multiple class periods face-to-face ILI scored significantly higher on tests than students who took an online tutorial (Nichols, Shaffer and Shockey, 2003).

One-shot ILI and accessing an ILI online tutorial will affect how a student learns. The one-shot face-to-face method is good for marketing or introducing the library and its resources to participants. The online tutorial will also deliver a familiarity level of knowledge and help increase a participant's research abilities. Neither of these methods will have a significant long term effect on a participant's critical thinking skills or a significant effect on their cognitive abilities. To make this type of impact the instruction needs to be more holistic, and should be face to face and include multiple sessions to have a long-term effect in life-long learning outcomes. ILI needs to be integrated across curriculums and offer extended experiences where the participants are exposed to the content more than once. Jennifer Jarson, an information literacy/assessment librarian at Muhlenberg College in Pennsylvania, claims: 'To achieve a sustained and significant impact, information literacy cannot be addressed only by librarians or only in isolated experiences' (Jarson, 2010). Cognitive skills and critical thinking develop over time from repeated exposure to different levels of content. Angela Weiler, a public services librarian at Onondaga Community College in Syracuse, New York, writes: 'Instructors and librarians would be well advised to keep in mind that cognitive ability is a developmental process and students must go through a series of steps over a period of time before they are able to seek information critically and reflectively' (Weiler, 2005). One-shot ILI and online tutorials are not going to affect a participant's cognitive ability in any significant way. ILI can be influential in changing the cognitive abilities and critical thinking skills if participants are presented with enough material and a sufficient number of experiences.

An active learning element should be considered a priority when the goal of ILI is to affect cognitive change. Chapter 2 showed that active learning is a more effective method of instruction than the traditional lecture method. A participant assessment will help determine whether a learner-centered instruction or a self-directed instruction would be more appropriate. Information processing needs considerable skill in the abstraction and significant cognitive development. To facilitate this type of learning, ILI needs to be designed in a continuum where participants are led through a series of lessons from simple search strategies to more complex ways of accessing and using information. An institution that selects cognitive changes as the objective or purpose of its program should look at designing multiple sessions, and face-to-face ILI that encourages interaction with the participant and the instruction.

## Affective changes

An ILI program that has an objective to create affective changes is looking to change a participant's emotions or attitudes toward task completion, and how much confidence participants have in their ability to complete a given task. The two most common experiences related to task performance using library skills are self-efficacy and library anxiety. Many participants have low levels of self-efficacy when faced with using the library. They do not feel they are capable or that they have the skills to find the information they need. Participants who have high levels of self-efficacy believe they can perform tasks well on their own. Participants who have a more positive attitude about using the library are confident they can do so. Library anxiety is the feeling of stress and disorientation when confronted with using the library. When faced with using library resources to fulfill information needs, most people in all types of libraries suffer from confusion and uncertainty, especially with difficult, complex information seeking assignments (Battle, 2004). ILI is used to increase participants' self-efficacy and decrease library anxiety.

To overcome affective characteristics requires a persuasive strategy and extended exposure. A combination of the strategies used in affecting behavioral and cognitive changes may be most effective for improving self-efficacy and lessening participants' anxious feelings about the library. Wen-Hua Ren, a librarian at Rutgers University, believes instruction not only needs to teach how to use the library, but should also change the way participants conceive the library. She wrote: 'It appears that library instruction would be most effective if it not only teaches the basic skills but also cultivates in the students a positive attitude and a strong motivation to continue to learn and practice those skills on their own' (Ren, 2000). In a research study, she measured increases in self-efficacy and decreases in library anxiety. She used a face-to-face ILI session that incorporated active learning elements and other modes of instruction to develop skills and reduce anxiety in a progression. She concluded that:

For self-efficacy to increase, students must have adequate searching practice, experience learning accomplishments and not be overwhelmed with negative emotions such as confusion and frustration. This calls for an accurate assessment of the students' level of search skills, on the basis of which, questions in the assignment are selected and sequenced according to levels of difficulty. Availability of practice facilities, encouraging searching environment and user-friendly point-of-use print and online instructional guides are also important contributors to gradual building up of self-efficacy. (Ren, 2000)

This is a blending of learning environments and methods to achieve a higher level of information literacy. It increases the cognitive skills of the participant and changes the attitude of the participant. This strategy will most likely promote life-long learning and provide changes that will be long term. The most effective method for producing affective changes is an FTF multiple-sessions ILI with an active learning element as well as print and online instruction to supplement additional learning experiences in a chronological progression. Table 4.1 shows the most effective ILI based on an organization's program objective.

Table 4.1  Selecting effective ILI method based on program objective

| Objective | ILI Method |
| --- | --- |
| Behavioral changes | FTF traditional lecture one-shot session |
| Cognitive changes | FTF active learning multiple sessions |
| Affective changes | FTF active learning multiple sessions |

# Choosing based on teaching method comparison

Chapter 2 listed a variety of successful pedagogical practices that can be incorporated into ILI: traditional lectures, active learning, computer assisted instruction, learner-centered instruction and self-directed independent learning. Each method has advantages and would prove most effective in specific situations. Traditional lectures are still the most popular ILI method used by all libraries. This section will choose the most effective method based on comparisons of the traditional method with the other methods available.

## *Traditional lecture vs active learning (AL)*

The effectiveness of traditional lectures has been questioned since the beginning of the instructional movement in libraries. Michael Lorenzen, an Illinois academic librarian, argues 'lecture may not be the most effective way of educating students about the library' (Lorenzen, 2001). He claimed that from the beginning of library instruction in the United States, it was noted that perhaps lecturing was not the most effective way of educating students about the library (Lorenzen, 2001). The research he was referring to also claimed there is a general assumption that lecturing limits student learning, and that a hands-on approach which involves active participation will increase student learning and retention (Johnson et al., 1991). Active participation engages the participants and helps them integrate instructional material that is new to them into the knowledge they already have (Burks and Hunt, 2003). Gary Phillips, an educational researcher, validated the well-known axiom, 'we remember

10 percent of what we hear, 15 percent of what we see, 20 percent of what we hear and see, 60 percent of what we do, and 80 percent of what we do with active reflection' (Phillips, 1984). Active learning is flexible; it incorporates a variety of learning styles which enables multiple learning style groups of participants to learn material in ways they would not if it was delivered in a lecture format (Burks and Hunt, 2003). And yet, a great part of instruction in libraries is still delivered in the traditional lecture despite the overwhelming evidence that alternative pedagogies can be more effective.

Numerous studies have shown that an active learning method does increase student learning and is more effective at increasing student learning than the traditional lecture method (Gradowski, Snavely and Dempsey, 1998; Walsh, 2010; Bren, 1998; Battle, 2004). *The Guidelines for Instructional Programs in Academic Libraries* developed and approved by the Association of College and Research Libraries suggests the use of active learning as a teaching strategy whenever possible. 'When possible, instruction should employ active learning strategies and techniques that require learners to develop critical thinking skills in concert with information literacy skills' (ACRL, 2003). The University of Wisconsin carried out a study to show that hands-on instruction is more effective than lecture/demonstration instruction for teaching research skills and concepts (Bren et al., 1998). The comparative study found that students who received the hands-on instruction had a greater retention level and performed better on the posttest than students who received the traditional lecture demonstration. The study suggests there is great value in hands-on instruction using a multi-station computer lab. Involving participants in their learning shares the responsibility of learning and has a greater impact on long-term retention and life-long learning (Wang, 2006). The importance of an active learning strategy in any ILI cannot be overstated. It works, and it works better than the traditional lecture method.

## *Traditional lecture vs computer-assisted instruction (CAI)*

Time constraints prevent extended access to participants, and most ILI is presented in a pre-scheduled one-hour period. Also, many facilities lack mediation in the rooms where the instruction is received. Librarians must choose how to best utilize the time and place they are restricted to, and present what they believe to be the most effective content based on their objectives of the instruction. CAI is possibly the most convenient method for users, especially participants who are distance learners or who do not have easy access to the library facilities. Not all participants have a computer or Internet access, and most CAI is delivered through web-based tutorials. Traditional lectures are most effective in all library environments when the facilities and time limit presentation. When there is no computer technology to allow active participation in the class, and class periods are limited to one hour, an informative lecture would be more beneficial than requiring the participants to introduce themselves to information literacy through a self-directed CAI method. Remote learners may be better served having access to a video of traditional instruction rather than only having access to CAI through web-based tutorials. CAI cannot provide the connectedness a participant feels in a traditional lecture instruction. It should not be considered a stand-alone instruction but can be beneficial as a supplement to other types of instruction (Tancheva, 2003). If limited to a choice between traditional lectures and

CAI, by comparison, the traditional lecture method will be more effective.

## Traditional lecture vs. learner-centered instruction (LCI)

Learner-centered instruction (LCI) is another interactive mode of instruction that involves the participants in the instruction. LCI is most suited for participant groups, where the members of each group support the learning experience by collaborating on knowledge construction between each other and the instructor. Grouping lends itself more to the academic library environment, though it is possible to transfer the strategy to both public and special libraries. This may support findings that LCI is rarely used (Walzyk and Ramsey, 2003). LCI requires a larger amount of effort and careful planning, but is well worth it. When it is used it is applied in all aspects of teaching and can be more effective than traditional lectures and increasing participant learning (Walzyk and Ramsey, 2003). LCI offers cognitive elements as well as affective ones, participants are excited about the content and look forward to learning, and it also communicates concern for student learning. LCI fosters intrinsic motivation, students feel good about their participation, and it is conceptually and in practice more effective for knowledge retention than traditional lecture learning (Walzyk and Ramsey, 2003; APA, 1997). LCI originates from the theory of constructivism. It acknowledges the active roles students must play in their learning if it is to occur deeply, to endure, be enjoyable, and transfer to contexts beyond the classroom (Walzyk and Ramsey, 2003). The LCI method works more effectively in the FTF environment than in the electronic environment. The connectedness and physical presence in the FTF class situation invite more interactivity between participants. Figure 1.8 presents an effective lesson plan for a single class period (90 minutes). This method is a better choice than traditional lecturing in many situations, including FTF one-shots, FTF for credit classes, and multiple class periods. It is an excellent choice for the lower levels of academic libraries (school and undergraduates), and would be highly beneficial in developing life-long lessons in information literacy.

## Traditional vs. self-directed independent learning (SDIL)

Self-directed learning takes a major commitment from the participant. A majority of participants are not used to being self directed learners. The growing popularity of distance learning and web-based instruction will require participants to become more familiar with a self-directed learning style. This method lends itself more to the electronic environment and web-based instruction. The participants are mainly on their own and have minimal contact with a librarian; they need to learn to expand the learning experience and complete tasks and research by themselves. There is evidence that SDIL can promote a higher level of student learning. A 1980s educational researcher named Mullen conducted a study that measured the effectiveness of independent learning. Mullen (1980) states that: 'There is convincing evidence that people who take the initiative in learning (proactive learners) learn more things, and learn better, than do people who sit at the feet of teachers passively waiting to be taught (reactive learners).' Though the SDIL method does develop higher learning skills in participants, it does not seem to be any more effective in increasing participant achievement of cognitive skills than traditional lectures. Alex Rodriguez, an educational researcher from the late 1990s, conducted a study that compared self-directed learning with traditional lecturing and found there was no significant difference between the two in increasing participant achievement. Rodriguez claimed, 'The independent study method when properly used, that is, when the professor using it knows how to use it, can develop in the students higher learning skills. It can give the students increased capability for generalization and transfer, a sense of the relevance of learning, and the ability to analyze, synthesize, and apply what is learned. In terms of student achievement, the independent study method does not seem to be more effective than other methods, as for example, the lecture method' (Rodriguez, 1998). This method is clearly more effective for distance learners in the electronic environment and is a good selection for online tutorials or other electronic instruction.

## Choosing based on learning-environment comparison

Finally, a decision based on learning environment. Since instruction has been offered through the Internet, studies have been comparing the FTF environment with the online environment in an attempt to see if there is a difference. The measurements have been cognitive, behavioral, and affective with very mixed results. There is little evidence that online instruction is more effective (Burkhardt, Kinnie and Cournoyer, 2008). Most of the studies devoted to comparisons between FTF and online IL instruction report no or little difference in student learning between the two methods (Russell, 1999; Germain et al., 2000; Holman, 2000; Kaplowitz and Contini, 1998; Gutierrez and Wang, 2001).

In many of the studies, librarians were available to help and supervise the participants as they took the tutorial, the posttest questionnaires were not the same for the control and experimental groups, and in some cases the tutorial was taken after a lecture by a librarian. All these confounding variables make the results of these studies questionable.

Two Australian librarian researchers, Marion Churkovich and Christine Oughtred, evaluated the instructional methods of Deakins University in an attempt to see which was more effective at increasing student learning outcomes. The study compared an online tutorial with the library's FTF instruction and strictly controlled the environments, methods, and confounding variables to validate their results. The researchers reported that students with FTF instruction gained higher posttest mean scores than students completing the online tutorial on their own. Additionally, students attending library sessions felt more confident about their library skills than those in the online tutorial-only sessions. Students who rated themselves poorly at finding library material in the pretest did much better in face-to-face classes than those who attended the mediated or tutorial groups, and the overall level of student confidence was significantly less for the tutorial-only delivery (Churkovich and Oughtred, 2002; Tancheva, 2003). Churkovich concluded, 'The results of our research indicate that contact with and instruction by a librarian is desirable for the best learning outcomes and confidence in development of information literacy skills. We attribute the success of the class group to flexible instruction, variety in presentation styles and reinforcement of concepts by a librarian' (Churkovich and Oughtred, 2002).

Arguably there is a difference, and for ILI, FTF is the more effective method for most situations. The instructional coordinator at Cornell University library, Kornelia Tancheva, performed a study that investigated the effectiveness of online tutorials, and through a literature review concluded that FTF is more effective than online instructions. She showed there is a significant difference, and in a 2003 article presents numerous studies that show FTF ILI lectures are more effective than online tutorials in many ways (Tancheva, 2003). At Cochise College in a formal poll of community college students, more than 70 percent would choose a FTF class over an online class if given the opportunity (Walsh, 2010). The students who participated had received both types of instruction and made their decisions based on a comparison of the two methods. The most often voiced reasons for choosing FTF were the structured format: they believed it was easier to keep focused and the physical environment kept them on track. Additionally, the students felt the access to the instructor was a significant advantage to student learning.

Online instruction cannot completely substitute for the connectedness of FTF instruction and should be used in connection with other academic methods, not in isolation (Dewald, 1999). Online tutorials are a good supplemental instruction, informative, and a good marketing tool. To affect the way a participant thinks and acts, to develop life-long learners who are truly information literate, will require the structure and connectedness offered by FTF instruction. Information literacy skills and critical thinking skills cannot be taught and absorbed in a single one-shot session of ILI. If the goal is to create an information literate society through instruction by librarians, the most effective method in any library environment is multiple session FTF active learning instruction that employs all types of supplemental instruction.

## Take-home message

The most significant factor to be considered when choosing an ILI method is the purpose or objective of your ILI program. FTF one shots are more appropriate for changing participant behavior; FTF multiple sessions are more effective in increasing cognitive outcomes and affective outcomes. There is no intention to have any method totally replace the traditional lecture. The lecture method can still be more effective than others in certain situations and does have its advantages. The lecture method is versatile and flexible. It is virtually limitless in application, either to situation, subject matter, or student age and learning ability. At the same time it can be one of the least effective methods if improperly used. The lecture method is more effective when visual aids, models, or some form of group participation is used (Rodriguez 1998). Each method should be utilized with a combination of approaches and should not be the sole method of teaching (Griffiths and Ursick, 2004). A blend of methods is always best if possible, and use of a variety of methods is always more effective than a single mode of instruction when trying to truly develop information literacy as a life-long learning skill. The Ren study measuring increases in self shows that college students' self-efficacy in electronic information searching was significantly higher after library instruction, which combined lecture, demonstration, hands-on practice, and an assignment of library electronic information searching (Ren, 2000).

Another important factor when selecting an ILI method is the participant. Grassian and Kaplowitz list knowing the audience as the number one rule in the rules for choosing an ILI method. They suggest that one solution for choosing an effective method of ILI is to develop specialized sessions that target each individual group of a participant population, but go on to mention that opportunities to teach targeted group sessions are very rare. Their recommendation is to vary and mix the ILI methods: 'No matter how you categorize your group differences, varying your methods and mixing the approaches increase the likelihood that you will reach all your participants regardless of their backgrounds' (Grassian and Kaplowitz, 2009). Participant populations will always be extremely diverse and one ILI method is not going to satisfy all of a population's needs. The library environment does vary; however, as has been said, a library is a library, is a library. Do not be too hasty in choosing an online tutorial; these should be considered supplemental instruction and combined with other instructional methods to contribute their full utility. So even though there are numerous factors to consider when choosing an effective ILI method, the most important ones to address first are the objective and the environment. Decide what you want to change in your participants. Do you want them to use the library more? Give them FTF one-shot active learning sessions. Do you want to increase their cognitive skills or change their attitudes? Provide multiple sessions of FTF active learning instruction. When libraries decided to be the leaders in the information literacy movement, their goal was the realization of an information literate society. To attain this goal and develop information literate participants will take an educational approach, not a marketing strategy. The best approach is to do it in a classroom, with librarians presenting the instruction. The advent of streamed video and conferencing software will bring this capability to the electronic environment through videos and blending of methods.

# References

American Psychological Association. (1997) Learner-centered Psychological Principles: A Framework for School Reform and Redesign. Available at *http://www.apa.org/index.aspx*.

Association of College and Research Libraries. (2003) The Guidelines for Instructional Programs in Academic Libraries. Available at *http://www.ala.org/ala/mgrps/divs/acrl/standards/guidelinesinstruction.cfm*.

Battle, J. (2004) The Effect of Information Literacy Instruction on Library Anxiety among International Students. (Doctoral dissertation, U of North Texas, May, 2004.) Proquest Information and Learning Company, 3126554.

Birks, J. and Hunt, F. (2003) *Hands-on Information Literacy Activities*. New York, NY: Neal-Schuman.

Bren, B., Hilleman, B. and Topp, V. (1998) Effectiveness of hands-on instruction of electronic resources. *Research Strategies*, 16(1): 41–51.

Burkhardt, J., Kinnie, J. and Cournoyer, C.M. (2008) Information Literacy Successes Compared: Online vs. Face to Face. *Journal of Library Administration*, 48(3/4): 379–89.

Center for Social Marketing and Behavioral Change. (2010) Ideas for Changing Lives. Available at *http://csmbc.aed.org/index.htm*.

Churkovich, M. and Oughtred, C. (2002) Can an Online Tutorial Pass the Test for Library Instruction? An Evaluation and Comparison of Library Skills Instruction Methods for First Year Students at Deakin University. *Academic and Research Libraries*, 33(1): 25–38.

Dewald, N., Scholtz-Crane, A. and Booth, H.A. (1999) Information Literacy at a Distance: Instructional Design

Issues. *Journal of Academic Librarianship*, 26(1): 33–44.

Germain, C.A., Jacobson, T. and Kaczor, S.A. (2000) A Comparison of the Effectiveness of Presentation Formats for Instruction: Teaching First-Year Students. *College and Research Libraries*, 6(1): 65–72.

Gradowski, G., Snavely, L. and Dempsey, P. (Eds) (1998) *Designs for Active Learning: A Sourcebook of Classroom Strategies for Information Education*. Chicago, IL: Association of College & Research Libraries.

Grassian, E. and Kaplowitz, J. (2009) *Information Literacy Instruction: Theory and Practice*. New York, NY: Neal-Schuman.

Griffiths, Y. and Ursick, K. (2004) Using Active Learning to Shift the Habits of Learning in the Health Care Education. *The Internet Journal of Allied Health Sciences and Practice*, 2(2): 1–5 Available at *http://ijahsp.nova.edu/articles/Vol2num2/pdf/griffiths.pdf*.

Gutierrez, C. and Wang, J.A. (2001) A Comparison of an Electronic vs. Print Workbook for Information Literacy Instruction at Richard Stockton College of New Jersey. *Journal of Academic Librarianship*, 27(3): 208–20.

Holman, L. (2000) A Comparison of Computer-assisted Instruction and Classroom Bibliographic Instruction. *Reference and User Services Quarterly*, 40(1): 53–65.

Jarson, J. (2010) Information Literacy and Higher Education; A Toolkit for Curricular Integration. *College and Research Libraries News*. Available at *http://crln.acrl.org/content/71/10/534.full*.

Johnson, D., Johnson, R. and Smith, K. (1991) *Active Learning: Cooperation in the college classroom*. Edina, MN: Interaction Books.

Kaplowitz, J.R. and Contini, J. (1998) Computer-assisted Instruction: Is It an Option for Bibliographic Instruction in Large Undergraduate Survey Classes? *College & Research Libraries*, 59: 19–28.

Kohl, D. and Wilson, L. (1986) Effectiveness of Course-integrated Bibliographic Instruction in Improving Course Work. *Reference Quarterly*, 26: 206–11.

Kunkel, L. and Weaver, S. (1996) What do They Know?: An Assessment of Undergraduate Library Skills. *Journal of Academic Librarianship*, 22: 430–5.

Lorenzen, M. (2001) Active learning and library instruction. Retrieved from *http://www.libraryinstruction.com/active.html*.

Madland, D. and Hagness, C. (1998) *The Case of Kelly*, in: G. Gradowski, L. Snavely and P. Dempsey (Eds), *Designs for Active Learning: A Sourcebook of Classroom Strategies for Information Education*, Association of College & Research Libraries, A Division of the American Library Association, Chicago, pp. 146–8.

Marcus, S. and Beck, S. (2003) A Library Adventure: Comparing a Treasure Hunt with a Traditional Freshman Orientation Tour. *College & Research Libraries*, 64: 23–44.

Mullen, R. (1980) *Working Papers on Contract Education*. ERIC ED 202 811.

Nichols, J., Shaffer, B. and Shockey, K. (2003) Changing the Face of Instruction: Is Online or In-class More Effective? *College and Research Libraries*, 64(5): 378–88.

Phillips, G. (1984) *Culture Shift*. Dallas, TX: Pritchett and Associates.

Portmann, C. and Roush, A. (2004) Assessing the effects of library instruction. *Journal of Academic Librarianship*, 30(6): 461–5.

Rangan, V., Karim, S. and Sandberg, S. (2009) Do Better at Doing Good. *Harvard Business Review*, 14(3): 1–12.

Ren, W. (2000) Library Instruction and College Student Self-efficacy in Electronic Information Searching. *The Journal of Academic Librarianship*, 26(5): 323–8.

Rodriguez, A.L. (ed.) (1998) *Comparison of Effectiveness of the Independent Learning Modality and Directed Classroom Modality at the Interamerican University.* Available at *http://ponce.inter.edu/cai/surisla/vol2/humani/comparis.htm*.

Russell, T.L. (1999) *The No Significant Difference Phenomenon as Reported in 355 Research Reports, Summary and Papers: A Comparative Research Annotated.* Bibliography on Technology for Distance Education. North Carolina State University.

Selegean, J.C., Thomas, M.L. and Richman, M.L. (1983) Long-range Effectiveness of Library Use Instruction. *College & Research Libraries*, 44(6): 476–80.

Small, R., Zakaria, N. and El-Figuigui, H. (2004) Motivational Aspects of Information Literacy Skills Instruction in Community College Libraries. *College and Research Libraries*, 96–120.

Tancheva, K. (2003) Online Tutorials for Library Instruction: An Ongoing Project under Constant Revision. Available at *http://www.ala.org/ala/mgrps/divs/acrl/events/pdf/tancheva.PDF*.

Walczyk, J. and Ramsey, L. (2003) Use of Learner-centered Instruction in College Science and Mathematics Classrooms. *Journal of Research in Science Teaching*, 40(6): 566–84.

Walsh, J. (2010) The Effects of Information Literacy Instruction on Student Library Usage. January 20, 2010. University of Arizona School of Information Resources and Library Science Lunch Lecture Series.

Wang, R. (2006) The Lasting Impact of a Library Credit Course. *Libraries and the Academy*, 6(1): 79–92.

Weiler, A. (2004) Information-Seeking Behavior in Generation Y Students: Motivation, Critical Thinking, and Learning Theory. *Journal of Academic Librarianship*, 31(1): 46–53.

# 5

# The future of information literacy instruction

**Abstract:** This chapter presents ideas and possibilities for ILI in the future. There is a need to expand the concept of information literacy to include a wider range of learning outcomes. The participants of the twenty-first century face a greater challenge, a greater risk, in searching for information. The Internet has changed the way that library participants search for information. They are more apt to fulfill their information needs without the epistemological protection a librarian provides. Participants will need to be educated about knowledge acquisition, and require a re-conceptualized ILI that changes the learning paradigm to promote multiple literacy skills: a multi-literacy instruction (MLI). This chapter introduces a concept for an MLI that combines two learning paradigms that teach IL skills and also the cyberliteracy skills needed to evaluate the types of information they would find using the Internet for their research. There is also a discussion of new direction for instruction in the face-to-face and electronic environment that would add functionality and applicability to existing online tutorials.

**Key words:** Multi-literacies, multi-literacy instruction, automated reference, disinformation, misinformation, information evaluation, cyberliteracy, online tutorials, re-conceptualized information literacy, information literacy pedagogy, information literacy learning paradigm, transliteracies.

## Multi-literacy instruction

Librarians were always the group of professionals that took responsibility for the reliability of information and protected their participants from the bad epistemic consequences caused by inaccurate information. This is no longer true. This was before current technology gave participants unlimited access to information on the Internet. The proportion of the world's population accessing online information continues to increase. According to Nielsen Rating, over 30 percent of the world's population used the Internet in 2010, up in the world by over 44 percent over the past ten years (Neilsen, 2010). A Pew Internet survey reports that 45 percent of U.S. Internet users make major life decisions based on information they acquire from the Internet (Horrigan, 2006). Library participants are using the Internet to acquire their information and making important decisions with it. They are acquiring knowledge from a media where anyone can write anything they want, true or false, anonymously and without consequences. This method of acquisition is threatening the epistemological protection librarians have provided. The problem is one of verifiability: the participants do not have a way to verify whether information is accurate or inaccurate. Inaccurate information is any misleading information. It can occur when information is incomplete or incorrect and happens through human error or outright lying. Inaccurate information can be unintentional or intentional and that is the difference between the subsets. Disinformation and misinformation are two different forms of inaccurate information (Fallis, 2009). Misinformation is inaccurate information created through honest mistakes and has no intention of misleading the user. The creation of disinformation is intentional and deliberately meant to mislead the user (Fallis, 2009).

The verification is even more difficult with disinformation. This type of inaccurate information is harder to identify because the creator wants to hide the fact that it is inaccurate (Fallis, 2009). Floridi claimed newspapers and television have already become 'instruments of disinformation' and believed the Internet would become a 'superhighway of disinformation' (Floridi, 1995). The Internet provides a perfect environment for disinformation. There are no quality control mechanisms to evaluate the content, no group of information and knowledge professionals to verify what sources are reliable and which ones are not. Brooks Jackson, the director of FactCheck.com and author of *Unspun, Finding Facts in a World of Disinformation*, calls the Internet 'a conduit of new gushers of toxic information sludge.' He claims disinformation is prevalent on the Internet and difficult to distinguish from the good stuff (Jackson, 2007). The recommended solutions for controlling disinformation by librarians fit into two categories, regulation and education.

There is a belief that library participants come to librarians to acquire knowledge and that knowledge is defined as true beliefs. Epistemology is the study of acquiring knowledge and epistemologists believe the generation of false beliefs from inaccurate information makes people worse off than they were before receiving the information. Therefore, this is considered one of the worst epistemic consequences (Fallis, 2008). Librarians have long been concerned with the epistemic consequences that library participants experience and protected them to make the consequences positive. Accurate and inaccurate information sit side by side and participants have no way to verify the accuracy. How can librarians help the participants verify information? Regulating the information on the Internet is not a plausible solution for librarians. In 2008 engineers at Google determined there were over a trillion unique URLs on the Internet, and the number of individual web pages out there grows by several billion pages per day (Alpert and Hajaj, 2008). Regulating information on the Internet is just not possible. As Rowan Pelling, a journalist for the *Telegraph UK*, wrote recently, 'Regulating the Internet is beyond mere mortals' (Pelling, 2008). Experts could not monitor existing sites nor keep up with the generation of new information and put their stamp of approval on all the accurate information.

Classification and organization are another solution mentioned, and warrant some investigation (Goldman in Fallis, 2004). Fallis claims it would be an effective way to help users verify inaccurate information (Fallis, 2006). Assuming it would also work on verifying disinformation, it could be a solution. This is something librarians have trusted experience in doing and it would not contradict our ethical principles. Before taking on this challenging task, many questions need answers. Is it something all would agree librarians should do? Is it a job for us? Who would be in charge? Where does the money come from to fund the project? What classification system do we use? These and many more decisions need to be made before classification can be considered. It qualifies ethically, but the ship may have sailed on this solution. If librarians had been in control of the net from the beginning we could have put users to work classifying each item they posted (Zhao, Plaisant and Shneiderman, 2001). Now, classification would be problematic; classifying what already exists would be a monumental challenge and questions the feasibility of this solution.

Mark Pendergrast, a librarian from Trinity College, reluctantly over 20 years ago suggested librarians start labeling disinformation when he identified inaccuracies of items on library shelves (Pendergrast, 1988). Don Fallis, a library science instructor from the University of Arizona, recommends we just verify inaccurate information for our users, which sounds a lot like labeling (Fallis, 2004). One of Floridi's possible solutions was something he called 'quality certification,' another name for labeling (Floridi, 1995). Then there is censorship, simply removing all the disinformation from the Internet (Fallis, 2009). Fallis recommends this as a less than effective solution for inaccurate information in general, and again assumed censorship would also work in controlling disinformation. The ethical and epistemic ramifications of censorship exclude it from consideration. It goes against librarians' basic ethical principles and there are 'epistemic costs to restricting access to information' (Fallis, 2004). Accurate information can be censored along with the inaccurate information and restricting plurality restricts the acquisition of true beliefs (Fallis, 2004). Any type of regulation needs extensive debate and extreme caution before implementation. Librarians stand for intellectual freedom and resisting censorship. These principles are the foundation of librarianship and do not integrate well with regulation of information. Librarians teach our participants how to acquire knowledge; they do not decide what knowledge they should acquire. Regulation, censorship, and labeling are unethical and should not be considered a feasible solution. Classification is ethical, just not feasible, but the sheer quantity of the information makes this method unrealistic. Education is the most viable solution. Controlling disinformation through education requires some foundational clarification. The ALA Presidential Committee on Information Literacy (IL) published an update in 1998 to its final report on IL from 1989. The report recommends 'that information literacy be promoted as a priority for all areas of education.' If librarians are going to solve this verifiability problem with education, it is going to be done by them using ILI. How can ILI help our participants with the verifiability problem? It is feasible and ethical, but is it an effective method for controlling disinformation?

Disinformation is harder to identify because the creator wants to hide the fact that it is inaccurate information and may require a different instructional technique (Fallis, 2009).

Chapter 1 defined information literacy as finding, evaluating, and using information effectively, and information literacy instruction (ILI) is teaching these skills depending on who is being taught and where the instruction takes place. The foundation of IL is to teach IL skills to participants so that they can become information literate and self-sufficient in acquiring and using information, in other words, to promote an information literate society. ILI developed in an effort to teach library users to be information literate. When ILI was conceptualized, the learning paradigm and learning objectives were sufficient. Whether the instruction is face to face or web delivered, whether it includes fully integrated classes, web-based tutorials or a one-shot session, the process always follows a scripted progression:

- Locate information using the library's resources and the Internet.
- Evaluate information using a list of information quality characteristics that usually indicate if it is reliable, quality information.
- Use information ethically and correctly.

Though not comprehensive, this strategy forms the basis for most web-based and face-to-face ILI. This pedagogical concept is not as effective in producing information literate participants for this ease-of-access, information-rich environment full of disinformation. There is no proven method to control disinformation and no way to protect participants from all that exists on the Internet. However, teaching them to become better 'epistemic justifiers' (Budd, 2004) may improve their chances of avoiding disinformation.

Developing better epistemic justifiers requires a re-conceptualized ILI learning paradigm that produces participants who are multi-literate. Studies have shown that in the current learning paradigm design, ILI is limited and requires additional elements to prepare participants for all the challenges they face when acquiring information. A 2008 study performed by a group of instructional researchers argued that the basic ILI pedagogy required modification (Hunt et al., 2008). The same study cited other research that recommended these changes: 'Initially, information literacy must be student-centered and account for multiple learning styles. Additionally, information literacy instruction must move away from the "show and tell" pedagogy and also teach e-research skills along with evaluation of sources and critical thinking skills' (Samson and Granath, 2001). Another study measuring the IL and IT competencies published in a 2003 book found deficiencies in the way ILI prepared participants: to address deficiencies in information literacy, educators must better understand how and why students gather information, and design instruction to determine '*what* students know, what they *think* they know, and what they *need* to know' (Stern, 2003). Participants will need additional skills to verify accurate information. So, how will librarians re-design the learning paradigm to help participants verify accurate information? To be a viable solution, the modifications should include an evaluation component that focuses on information accuracy. There should also be a change in the learning paradigm that allows for a more skeptical approach to acquiring knowledge. The new ILI would create a multi-literacy instruction (MLI) that combines multiple disciplines into one instructional process.

The evaluation element is the part of ILI pedagogy that can help with the verifiability problem, but it needs more accurate evaluation indicators. Librarians employ a standard method in ILI for evaluating information on the Internet. Most often the method involves an explanation of information quality characteristics that help the student identify quality information. There is a set of widely accepted standard guidelines used as indicators of accurate information (Smith, 1997). Verifying information about the information shows whether the indicators are present or not. Who is the author of the page? Is there contact information for the author? Was the author qualified to write the page? These are the types of questions asked when verifying accuracy. When was the page last updated? Are there any dead links on the page? Is the information outdated? These would be questions to verify currency (Kapoun, 1998). Table 5.1 lists the evaluation indicators, the questions a participant would ask about the indicators, and the basic analysis of the answers. The current

**Table 5.1** Evaluation criteria for internet information

| Evaluation of web documents | How to interpret the basics |
| --- | --- |
| 1. Accuracy of web documents | Accuracy |
| Who wrote the page and can you contact him or her? | Make sure author provides an e-mail or a contact address/phone number. |
| What is the purpose of the document and why was it produced? | Know the distinction between author and webmaster. |
| Is this person qualified to write this document? | |
| 2. Authority of web documents | Authority |
| Who published the document and is it separate from the 'Webmaster'? | What credentials are listed for the authors? |
| Check the domain of the document: what institution publishes this document? | Where is the document published? Check URL domain. |
| Does the publisher list his or her qualifications? | |

3. Objectivity of web documents

What goals/objectives does this page meet?

How detailed is the information?

What opinions (if any) are expressed by the author?

Objectivity

Determine if page is a mask for advertising; if so information might be biased.

View any web page as you would an infommercial on television. Ask yourself: why was this written and for whom?

4. Currency of web documents

When was it produced?

When was it updated?

How up-to-date are the links (if any)?

Currency

How many dead links are on the page?

Are the links current, or updated regularly?

Is the information on the page outdated?

5. Coverage of web documents

Are the links (if any) evaluated and do they complement the document's themes?

Is it all images or a balance of text and images?

Is the information presented cited correctly?

Coverage

If page requires special software to view the information, how much are you missing if you don't have the software?

Is it free or is there a fee to obtain the information?

Is there an option for text only, or frames, or a suggested browser for better viewing?

**Putting it all together**

**Accuracy.** If your page lists the author and institution that published the page and provides a way of contacting him/her and . . .

**Authority.** If your page lists the author credentials and its domain is preferred (.edu, .gov, .org, or .net), and . . .

**Objectivity.** If your page provides accurate information with limited advertising and it is objective in presenting the information, and . . .

**Currency.** If your page is current and updated regularly (as stated on the page) and the links (if any) are also up-to-date, and . . .

**Coverage.** If you can view the information properly – not limited to fees, browser technology, or software requirement, then . . .

You may have a web page that could be of value to your research!

*Source*: Kapoun (1998)

accuracy evaluation indicators are not necessarily the best indicators of accuracy for web-based information. In his article 'Verifying the Accuracy of Information,' Don Fallis applies epistemology to the problem of verifying accuracy of information. He provides a conceptual framework in the article that explains the effectiveness of the standard guidelines librarians use for evaluating information (Fallis, 2004). The article also explains that the guidelines used are not scientifically tested. Two studies tested the guideline characteristics and indicate that the evaluation indicators of quality and accuracy of web pages do not correlate with accuracy (Fallis and Fricke, 2002; Frick and Fallis, 2004). New indicators of accuracy are just one of the changes the ILI learning paradigm needs to make it more effective for today's participants.

Librarians also have to change the epistemology of ILI and its relationship with critical thinking (Lankshear, 2000). The learning paradigm follows that the user recognizes a problem, finds information, evaluates and organizes the information in a way to solve the problem, and then uses the information to solve the problem. This concept of critical thinking is associated with foundationalism (Kapitzke, 2003). Foundationalism is an epistemological theory involving the justification of beliefs and how we justify or believe what we know (Fumerton, 2005). Cushla Kapitzke, a Behavioral Science professor from the University of Queensland, calls this approach to information 'operational' (Kapitzke, 2003). She contends that this allows the student to 'learn information through information, but the student does not learn anything about information and knowledge' (Kapitzke, 2003). This paradigm does not encourage enough critical reflection about the information (Kapitzke, 2003). The user is not skeptical enough. The lack of reliable accuracy indicators and an epistemic weakness in the ILI learning paradigm are design flaws. Kapitzke's suggestion of the creation of a 'hyperliteracy' inspired the idea of combining literacies. Information literacy skills are no longer sufficient to prepare participants to acquire knowledge in their preferred method. Educating participants needs to go beyond developing just IL skills, and participants must be taught to be more skeptical.

First, the epistemic weakness of the learning paradigm can be fixed by introducing skepticism. Librarians need to find a literacy that is based on skepticism and combine it with ILI to create a new multi-literacy instructional (MLI) method that is more skeptical. The new method would be designed around the types of information our users are accessing in the twenty-first century, including disinformation on the Internet. Additionally, the evaluation process requires a new focus. The ILI process focuses on evaluating information with a set of criteria, one of which is accuracy. The new process will focus on evaluating the accuracy of the information. MLI will form a new strategy with a different learning paradigm and an evaluation component that has accuracy indicators proven in providing accurate information. There are still some unanswered questions. How does epistemology help? What is the new literacy? What will change? What are the new accuracy indicators? What would MLI look like? What are the evaluation criteria? Let's start by explaining why epistemology is important.

The ALA Presidential Committee on Information Literacy promotes ILI as a 'means of personal empowerment' because it allows people to become 'seekers of truth.' IL also allows people 'to experience the excitement of the search for knowledge and their own successful quest for knowledge' (Lapitzke, 2003; ALA, 1989/1998). If ILI empowers users to find truths and acquire knowledge, the objectives of ILI are epistemic. Using Internet information and verifying accurate information introduces new learning into the pedagogy of ILI, and epistemology can help to meet that objective. Table 5.2 shows a comparison of the learning objectives defined by the Association of College and Research Libraries (ACRL) in their *Competency Standards for Information Literacy* and a new set of learning objectives designed for MLI. ILI is associated with the epistemic theory of foundationalism. Foundationalism theorizes that what we know or believe comes from basic beliefs or self-evident beliefs and that justification for these beliefs is internal (Fumerton, 2005). Lapitzke believes this concept does not encourage the user to critically reflect enough about the information. There is a lack of skepticism. Skepticism is associated with the epistemology theory of reliablism (Hooker, 1996). The theory of reliablism claims that we justify true beliefs only through a reliable cognitive process,

Table 5.2  Learning objectives

| Information literacy | Mutli-literacy |
| --- | --- |
| Determine a need for information | Acquire a familiarity with basic information technology hardware and software |
| Access the needed information | |
| Evaluate information critically | Learn to receive and transmit digital information |
| Use information effectively | |
| Use information ethically and legally | Identify the need for information |
| | Understand issues associated with the Internet |
| | Detect the dangers of the Internet and protect yourself against them |
| | Find information using a variety of resources |
| | Verify the accuracy of information |
| | Organize information and use it to fulfill need |
| | Understand the economic, legal, and social issues surrounding the use of information. |

## The future of information literacy instruction

and that justification for these beliefs is external (Hayden, 2008). We justify B only if B has been arrived at through a reliable process. Reliablism inspired skepticism, and according to skepticism knowledge is only acquired through doubt and scrutiny (Hooker, 1996).

ILI is associated with foundational concepts and is not skeptical enough to teach participants how to avoid disinformation. So do librarians change to a literacy instruction that is associated with reliablism and teach from a learning paradigm of skepticism? If a critical thinking paradigm is too credulous, would a skepticism paradigm not be too skeptical? Would participants then be to skeptical to determine the difference between the accurate and inaccurate information? Librarians want the users to be skeptical enough to investigate for evidence in order to verify the information, but not so skeptical that they would ignore accurate information in their quest for verification. How do we obtain equilibrium? The answer is to combine some literacy with a skeptical learning paradigm together with the critical thinking paradigm of ILI and form a new multi-literacy (ML) learning paridigm. Cyber literacy is based on a critical literacy paradigm and may contain the element of skepticism required (Stiller, 2006; Gregson, 2008).

Laura Gurak, a nationally recognized Internet researcher, defines cyberliteracy as 'a set of concepts and critical views with which to understand today's Internet' (Gurak, 2003). She calls it a newly emerging electronic literacy that employs a special form of critical thinking which takes a more critical perspective about Internet technology. Gurak wrote a book called *Cyberliteracy: Navigating the Internet with Awareness*. The book lays out a framework for developing a literacy that teaches people how to be cyber literate. Gurak describes a person who is cyber literate as 'someone who understands the relationship between our communication technologies, our communities and our cultures' (Gurak, 2003). Cyber literacy teaches a set of competencies that introduce more skeptical learning objectives. The competencies are based on critical literacy. Critical literacy has been described as a critical questioning of media expressions, especially electronic media (Tyner, 1998). Barbara Warnick, a professor of Rhetorical Criticism, describes critical literacy 'as a focus on making what is hidden or not apparent in communications visible.' Warnick describes the following list of items as techniques that would help someone become cyber literate:

- recognizing that media discourse is often persuasive in nature;
- questioning the motives, ideology, and values of the authors of a communication;
- identifying the genre (e.g. exhortation, parodic commentary, epideictic speech, predictive narrative, etc.) of a communication;
- identifying the form of argument (e.g. argument from model, dissociation, and analogy) embodied in a communication;
- identifying the beliefs, values, and assumptions that are assumed by the authors of a communication to be held by the audience.

The characteristics of this set of objectives are more critical and skeptical than the learning objectives defined in the ACRL's *Competency Standards for Information Literacy*. Evelyn Stiller and Cathie LeBlanc are computer science instructors at Plymouth State University in New Hampshire. They have designed and implemented a cyber literacy course using the concepts from Gurak's book and Warnick's critical literacy techniques. They created a list of competencies (see Table 5.3) that address issues associated with Internet communications and the dangers associated with the Internet (Stiller, 2006). Combining these competencies with the critical thinking competencies increases the skepticism of the ILI paradigm. Critical literacy and critical thinking combine both internal and external epistemic justification concepts creating a more skeptical learning paradigm. MLI has a learning paradigm more suitable for dealing with disinformation and developing the skills for finding, verifying and using Internet information. Now the ILI evaluation component needs more effective accuracy indicators.

The evaluation element will no longer focus on the information – it will focus on the accuracy of the information. Table 5.4 shows a new set of MLI evaluation criteria that have been scientifically tested and are more likely to correlate

**Table 5.3**  Cyber literacy course: competencies

| |
|---|
| 2.0 Keeping up with current events |
| 2.1 Expressing oneself politically, creatively, and artistically |
| 2.2 Finding students' voices |
| 2.3 Artists' notes and journals |
| 2.3.1 Student web logs |
| 2.4 E-mail and other electronic transactions |
| 2.5 Understanding the ethical and social issues connected with web-based information |
| 2.5.1 Intellectual property |
| 2.5.2 Libel |
| 2.5.3 Netiquette |
| 2.5.4 Media ownership |
| 2.6 Virtual communities |
| 2.7 Understanding the dangers of the Internet |
| 2.8 Understanding privacy issues on the Internet |
| 2.9 Diversity and the Internet |
| 3.0 Accessibility and the Internet |

Source: Stiller (2006)

# Information Literacy Instruction

**Table 5.4** MLI accuracy evaluation criteria

| Evaluation of accuracy | How to interpret accuracy |
|---|---|
| **Source accuracy** | **Source** |
| Who wrote the page/is there contact information? | Make sure author provides email or contact information |
| What is the purpose of this information? | Know the distinction between author and webmaster |
| Is the person qualified to write this information? (Kapoun, 1998) | Use link structure of information or web to verify information |
| **Currency accuracy** | **Currency** |
| How recently was the page updated? | Information is clearly dated |
| Are there any dead links? | Information gives regularity of updates |
| Is the information outdated? | Information has date of copyright |
| **Copyright accuracy** | **Copyright** |
| Is the information copyrighted? | Copyright claim is clearly displayed |
| **Link structure accuracy inlinks** | **Inlinks** |
| How many inlinks were found to the website? | The higher the number of inlinks the more likely the information is accurate. (To determine inlink quantity type 'link:websit-url' into Google). |
| **Link structure accuracy PageRank** | **Google PageRank** |
| Is the Google PageRank greater than 5? | Use the Google PageRank tool at http://www.prchecker.info/check_page_rank.php. |

**Putting it all together**

**Source accuracy.** If the information lists the author and institution that published the page and provides a way of contacting him/her and . . .

**Currency accuracy.** If the information is clearly dated, has a copyright date or regularity update information, has no dead links and . . .

**Copyright accuracy.** If the information has a copyright claim, and . . .

**Inlink accuracy.** If the information has a high number of inlinks and . . .

**PageRank accuracy.** If the information has a Google PageRank greater than 5 then . . .

**You may have accurate information!**

*Source:* Walsh (2010)

with accuracy than the traditional set of IL indicators. There is no empirical evidence which shows that certain accuracy indicators can help in the verification of disinformation on the Internet. There is empirical evidence showing that the indicators in Table 5.4 are indicators of accuracy for health information and reference questions from the Internet (Fallis and Fricke, 2002; Fallis and Fricke, 2004). The study found that if the indicators were present, a website would be more likely to contain accurate information (Fallis and Fricke 2004). These are the only proven indicators of accuracy and are assumed to be valid for use in MLIs evaluation process. There were four accuracy indicators proven most likely to return accurate information: currency, copyright, inlinks, and Google PageRank (Fallis and Fricke, 2004). Inlinks is the number of websites that link to a website (Fallis and Fricke, 2004). To find the number of inlinks to a particular website you just type 'link:website_url' into the Google search box. For instance, to find the number of links coming into the University of Arizona website, type link:arizona.edu into the search box (Roy, 2001). Google PageRank is another link structure indicator that uses the number of inlinks and other criteria in an algorithm that evaluates the importance of a webpage. It is done by using the Google PageRank Checker (PR Checker, 2009). These indicators and the standard accuracy indicator from ILI will make up the evaluation criteria for MLI. MLI now has a pedagogy that could be effective in preparing participants for the challenges they face in today's information world and are effective in verifying disinformation.

Multi literacy is:

> the ability to recognize a problem, know how to recognize and address issues associated with Internet communications, know and recognize the dangers associated with the Internet, find information to solve the problem, evaluate the accuracy of the information, organize the information to solve the problem, use the information to solve the problem.

The above model is basic, but functional. The learning paradigm includes critical thinking components and critical literacy components. The objectives reflect the skepticism of critical literacy. The MLI evaluation criteria have a similar structure to ILI, except that the focus is on the evaluation of accuracy. Lesson plans could include the importance of keeping up with current events, the dangers and issues involved with all communications on the Internet, the ethical and social issues connected with web-based information, the different types of inaccurate information you can encounter, and how to verify the accuracy of information on the Internet.

MLI is structured to educate participants about the different kinds of information available in the twenty-first century and how to find it, verify it, and use it. Whether it works or not remains to be seen. Determining effectiveness requires design and implementation of lesson plans that target prospective audiences, and then an assessment and evaluation process needs to be done. After extended use and modification, experimental research needs to be done to measure the effectiveness. Another consideration to take into account is the old adage about leading a horse to water, but. . . Teaching participants how they ought to do something and having them do it is not always the progression of reality (Fallis, 2004). MLI should make our participants better 'epistemic justifiers,' and more skeptical of the information they access on the Internet. This combination will more likely than not develop multi-literate participants who have the necessary skills to complete 'their own successful quest for knowledge.'

A prototype software exists that can verify information accuracy using some of the proven accuracy indicators mentioned (Price and Hersh, 1999). This type of technology will probably be the most effective method available to participants for finding and using Internet information in the future. The concept of a multi-literacy instructional model and its usefulness to librarians may have a longer duration. Joan Kaplowitz, co-writer of *Information Literacy Instruction, Theory and Practice*, believes instruction is the future of librarianship. The technology of information and new resources is growing at an exponential rate. Kaplowitz claims instruction of some kind will continue to be needed (Kaplowitz, 2009). MLI has the potential to advance the careers of librarians. Many librarians are already doing a form of MLI in all types of libraries. More than 35 percent of all reference questions received at Cochise College Libraries Douglas campus over the 2009/10 academic year were technology related (Walsh, 2010). The skills librarians are teaching through individual reference sessions should be combined with the class sessions of ILI. MLI is flexible and can be combined with any literacy to form a new learning paradigm to meet whatever the learning objectives happen to be. This is similar to the concept introduced at the University of California, Santa Barbara in

2005 called transliteracies. Transliteracy combines literacies (digital literacy, media literacy, information literacy, visual literacy, twenty-first-century literacies) to form a learning paradigm that teaches the ability to read, write, and interact with information across all existing platforms. In other words, a transliterate person is one who is literate in multiple media.

## Transliteracies

The concept of transliteracy has been around for centuries, developing from the ability to write or print in multiple alphabets. The updated meaning of the term transliteracies evolved at the Transcriptions Research Project directed by Professor Alan Liu in the Department of English at the University of California Santa Barbara in 2005. *Transliteracy* is a recent terminology gaining currency in the library world. Transliteracy is the ability to read, write, and interact across a range of platforms, tools, and media from signing and orality through handwriting, print, TV, radio, and film, to digital social networks (Transliteracies Project, 2010). The concept is not library-centric and is not familiar to most in librarianship. Consequently, the term is not often related with the information literacy instructional mission librarians have been supporting. The term is still new; it is still in flux and has not been fully defined. Transliterate will be what it means to be literate in the twenty-first century. It is an inclusive concept which bridges and connects past, present and, hopefully, future modalities (Thomas et al., 2007). A group of academics at the Institute of Creative Technologies, De Montfort University are working to identify transliteracies and examples of transliterate practice. Sue Thomas is the coordinator and the group formed the

Production and Research in Transliteracy (PART) in 2006. They support ideas about media convergence held by MIT scholar Henry Jenkins: 'While it can be easy to tie transliteracy to technology, transliteracies are not just about computer-based materials, but about all communication types across time and culture and include technological, economic, social, cultural, and global issues' (Thomas et al., 2007). This is an opportunity for librarians to help in the development and conceptualization of transliteracies and become leaders in the movement. Librarians should not just be watching developments in this new field, they should be involved in the development and make known how transliteracies instruction will impact participants. Librarians are uniquely positioned to be the leaders in the transliteracies movement. Libraries and librarians already play an important role in the education of people for effective and efficient information use by teaching them information skills at all levels of education. They are key personnel in the implementation of resource-based programs. They are designers of the information literacy curriculum and have expertise in this field. They have always been leaders in new information technologies and have the experience with information-finding tools that gives them a context for the application of new tools such as the different media of the World Wide Web (Dhiman, 2006). Librarians are good educators and have the skill set to educate participants in multiple literacies. This should be promoted at the educational level of librarians, and all Library Science graduate programs should introduce more advanced instructional requirements for their students. Librarians are spending more and more of their everyday schedule on instruction and this should be reflected in the education of future librarians.

# Other new ideas for ILI

## *Fully automated reference instruction (FARI)*

'Most researchers argue that online tutorials should be used as supplements' (Tricarico et al., 2001, in Tancheva, 2003) or at least combined with face-to-face instruction. 'That is, online tutorials are seen as more of a complement or a tool of supplementary instruction rather than as an effective stand-alone teaching tool' (Tancheva, 2003). Most online tutorials provide a drill-and-practice system with no applicable simulation learning and are not considered effective as a point-of-need instructional tool. If there is simulation, it is usually limited and mostly predefined to searches that do not simulate the true experience of searching for resources. When online tutorials were conceived, one of the key features that made them so attractive was point-of-need access capabilities. It is questionable whether participants even look to an online tutorial for point-of-need instruction when they are involved in a project that requires research. According to a study done at the University of Minnesota Library (Veldof and Beavers, 2001), the majority of their research study participants made it clear that they would not be likely to use the tutorial unless it were incorporated into a course curriculum, grading, and instructor expectations (Tancheva, 2003). The best way to make online tutorials into an instructional tool that provides the same degree of concept-teaching, interactivity, and active collaborative learning centered on the user, and that has point of need capability, is to design a full blown simulation software – a simulation that provides the true search experience by having the participant progress through the search strategy while using the search engine or database that is best suited for the assignment at hand. A fully automated reference instruction (FARI) or 'The Reference Fairy,' walks the participant along a progressive step-by-step search in a database that provides resources related to the specific subject and topic of their choice. An animated interface takes the participant through the search cycle, starting with defining their need for information, developing keywords for search terms through an interactive thesaurus of terms in psychology or allowing the participant to input terms. The participant would then be prompted through choosing the correct database from a list of psychology databases of APA journals. Eventually the participant would be prompted through the search process using the database. These will not be predefined searches, but a search using the keywords developed by the participant. The technology already exists for student-centered full-blown simulation search. Microsoft has a prototype of a virtual assistant called Laura that is a talking head and lives on the desktop of your PC. The software has sophisticated decision-making capabilities based on a personal profile of real-life and computer activities (Hodgin, 2009). This type of technology will probably be the most effective method for directing participants through their daily informational needs.

## Social psychology and ILI

Another idea that deserves some consideration when designing an effective ILI method is the combination of social psychology concepts with library instruction. Social psychology has developed a theory of how people receive and route information after reception. When people are given information, they assign it a priority and then route it in their brain in a certain way depending on the priority it is assigned, and that affects how they act on the information. For example, when people are given information that they consider low priority they route it peripherally; if they assign it a high priority they route it centrally. When information is routed peripherally, the participant will have a low impact reaction to the information. The information is classified in a generalized or generic category and it becomes just an activity and something to get finished as soon as possible; i.e. participants will act differently on an assignment of a research paper than they would if they are given information on a health problem or if they are going to spend money on something. Information about a health problem of personal economics is the kind of information a participant will route centrally and assign it a high priority, checking out numerous resources, asking different people who know about the information, and participants do not care how much time or effort is expended on the task. Centrally routing is conducive to critically understanding the information and long-term retention (Rafindadi, 2010). Centrally routing information is not a skill that can be taught, but you can persuade participants to do this (Rafindadi, 2010). Persuasion is used in marketing all the time to convince people to centrally route information (Rafindadi, 2010). Since one of the main objectives of ILI is to market the resources, an instructional method that employs an element of persuasion seems most appropriate. The foundation of a persuasive technique is in the delivery of the instruction. Successful marketers in everything from consumer products to politics have used expertise to present 'sell' information. The hosts are most convincing if they possess expert knowledge in the field and can persuade the participants that they have expert knowledge.

## Take-home message

The proliferation of information resources, due to rapid technological changes and easier access to resources via the

Internet, has complicated the ways in which library participants acquire information (American Association of College and Research Libraries, 2000; Swanson, 2004; Wilder, 2005). This change in knowledge acquisition behavior has increased the importance of information fluency and the demand for ILI. It is rapidly becoming a key component of general education programs (Jacobson and Mark, 2000) and, in most libraries, of public service offerings. The new behavior calls for an expansion of the fundamental skills required to be considered information literate. Meeting these progressive needs may require a re-conceptualization of IL and how it is taught. One solution is to combine the concepts and learning paradigms of multiple literacies to form a dynamic pedagogy that changes with time and technology, always teaching the most relevant skills. A multi-literacy instruction allows for flexibility and shifts in the learning objectives and paradigms. This type of instructional method could be effective in maintaining the pace with information technology and supporting the life-long learning concept. MLI would be a developmental literacy, changing over a library participant's lifetime, teaching whatever required skills were needed. Online tutorials also need fundamental re-structuring. The face-to-face environment is more desirable than the electronic environment for the best learning outcomes and confidence in development of information literacy skills (Churkovich and Oughtred, 2002). ILI online tutorials will be considered as supplemental instruction until they can deliver the connectedness and point of need instruction that FTF instruction supplies. The most effective solution would be to develop a full blown real-time search simulation tutorial that supports live participant interaction as the instruction leads the participant through the research cycle. Finally, participants can be taught to route instructional information in a certain way that promotes critical analysis of information and long-term retention. To be more effective in teaching participants, librarians should consider employing the social psychology concepts and persuasive techniques in the design of ILI.

# References

Alpert, J. and Hajaj, N. (2008) We knew it was big ... Google Blog. Accessed 22 March 2009 at *http://googleblog.blogspot.com/2008/07/we-knew-web-was-big.html.*

American Library Association. (1989) *American Library Association on Information Literacy.* Available at *http://www.ala.org/ala/mgrps/divs/acrl/publications/whitepapers/presidential.cfm.*

American Library Association. (1998) *A Progress Report on Information Literacy: An Update on the American Library Association Presidential Committee on Information Literacy: Final Report.* Chicago: ALA, American Library Association. Available at *http://www.ala.org/ala/mgrps/divs/acrl/publications/whitepapers/progressreport.cfm.*

American Library Association. (2005) *Resolution on Disinformation, Media Manipulation, & the Destruction of Public Information.* Available at *http://bc.barnard.columbia.edu/~jfreedma/ALA/disinformation.pdf.*

Association of College and Research Libraries (ACRL). (2010) *Competency Standards for Information Literacy in Higher Education.* Available at *http://www.ala.org/ala/mgrps/divs/acrl/standards/informationliteracycompetency.cfm.*

Budd, J. (2004) Academic Libraries and Knowledge: A Social Epistemology Framework. *The Journal of Academic Librarianship*, 30(5): 361–7.

Dhiman, A.K. (2006) *Information Literacy and the Role of the Librarian.* Available at *http://ir.inflibnet.ac.in/dxml/bitstream/handle/1944/1207/42.pdf?sequence=1.*

Fallis, D. (2004) On Verifying the Accuracy of Information: Philosophical Perspectives. *Library Trends*, 52(3). 463–87.

Fallis, D. (2006) Social Epistemology and Information Science. *Annual Review of Information Science and Technology*. Vol. 40, ed. Blaise Cronin. Medford, NJ: Information Today, 475–519.

Fallis, D. (2008) Toward an Epistemology of Wikipedia. *Journal of the American Society for Information Science and Technology*, 59: 1662–74.

Fallis, D. (2009) *A Conceptual Analysis of Disinformation*. Available at *http://sirls.arizona.edu/files/14/fallis_disinfo.pdf*.

Fallis, D. and Frické, M. (2002) Indicators of Accuracy of Consumer Health Information on the Internet: A Study of Indicators Relating to Information for Managing Fever in Children in the Home. *Journal of the American Medical Informatics Association*, 9(1), 73–9.

Floridi, Luciano. (1996) *Brave.Net.World: The Internet as a Disinformation Superhighway?* Available at *http://www.philosophyofinformation.net/publications/pdf/bnw.pdf*.

Frické, M. and Fallis, D. (2004) Indicators of Accuracy for Answers to Ready Reference Questions on the Internet. *Journal of the American Society for Information Science and Technology*, 55, 238–45.

Fumerton, R. (2005) *Foundationalist Theories of Epistemic Justification. Stanford Encyclopedia of Philosophy*. Available at *http://plato.stanford.edu/entries/justep-foundational/*.

Goldman, A.I. (1999) *Knowledge in a social world*. New York: Oxford University Press.

Gregson, S. (2008) *Cyber Literacy: Evaluating the Reliability of Data*. New York: Rosen Publishing Group.

Gurak, L. (2003) *Cyberliteracy: Navigating the Internet with Awareness*. New Haven, CT: Yale University Press.

Hodgin, R. (2009) Microsoft Working on Bob 2.0? Meet Laura the talking head. *Tech Generation Daily*. Available at *http://www.tgdaily.com/content/view/41600/113/*.

Hooker, R. (1996) *Skepticism*. World Civiliazations, Available at *http://wsu.edu/~dee/GLOSSARY/SKEPT.HTM*.

Horrigan, J. and Rainie, L. (2006) *When Facing a Tough Decision, 60 Million Americans Now Seek the Internet's Help; The Internet's Growing Role in Life's Major Moments*. Pew Research Center Publication, Pew Internet and American Life Project. Available at *http://pewresearch .org/pubs/19/when-facing-a-tough-decision-60-million-americans-now-seek-the-internets-help*.

Hunt, S.K., Novak, D.R., Semlak, J.L. and Meyer, K.R. (2005) Synthesizing the first 15 years of the Basic Communication Course Annual: What research tells us about effective pedagogy. *Basic Communication Course Annual*, 17: 1–42.

Jackson, B. and Jamieson, K.H. (2007) *unSpun: Finding Facts in a World of Disinformation*. New York: Random House.

Jacobson, T.E. and Mark, B.L. (2000) Separating Wheat from Chaff: Helping First-Year Students Become Information Savvy. *Journal of General Education*, 49: 256–78.

Jenkins, H. (2001) Convergence? I diverge. *Technology Review*. Available at *http://www.technologyreview.com/ Biztech/12434/*.

Kapitzke, C. (2003) Information Literacy: a Positivist Epistemology and a Politics of Outformation. *Educational Theory*, 53(1): 37–53.

Kapoun, J. (July/August 1998) Teaching undergrads WEB evaluation: A guide for library instruction. *C&RL News*: 522–3.

Kasowitz-Scheer, A. and Pasqualoni, M. (2002) *Information Literacy Instruction in Higher Education: Trends and Issues*. ERIC Clearinghouse on Information and Technology, Syracuse, NY. Available at *http://searcheric.org/digests/ed465375.html*.

Lankshear, C., Snyder, I. and Breen, B. (2000) *Teachers and Technoliterac: Managing Literacy, Technology and Learning in Schools*. New South Wales: Allen and Unwin.

Meyer, K.R., Hunt, S.K., Hopper, K.M., Thakkar, Kashmira V., Tsoubakopoulos, V. and Van Hoose, K.J. (2008) Assessing Information Literacy Instruction in the Basic Communication Course. *Communication Teacher*, 2(1): 22–34.

Neilsen Ratings. (2010) United States of America Internet Usage and Broadband Usage Report. *Internet World Stats*. Available at *http://www.internetworldstats.com/am/us.htm*.

Pelling, R. (2008) Regulating the Internet is Beyond mere Mortals like Sir Tim Birners-Lee. Telegraph.co.uk. Accessed 16 March 2009 at *http://www.telegraph.co.uk/comment/personal-view/3562217/Regulating-the-internet-is-beyond-mortals-like-Sir-Tim-Berners-Lee.html*.

Pendergrast, M. (1988) In Praise of Labeling; or, When shalt Thou Break Commandments? *Library Journal*, 113(10): 83–5.

Price, S. and Hersh, W. (1999) *Filtering Web Pages for Quality Indicators: An Empirical Approach to Finding High Quality Consumer Health Information on the World Wide Web*. Available at *http://www2.amia.org/pubs/symposia/D005524.PDF*.

Rafindadi, K. (2010) M.D. Psychology, personal interview conducted at Cochise College.

Samson, S. and Granath, K. (2001) Information literacy and the academy. *The Montana Professor*, 11(2): 15–17.

Smith, A. (1997) *Testing the Surf: Criteria for Evaluating Internet Information*. VUW Department of Library and Information Studies, New Zealand. Available at *http://www.vuw.ac.nz/staff/alastair_smith/evaln/*.

Stern, C.M. and Rader, H. (eds) (2003) *Measuring students' information literacy competency. Information and IT literacy: Enabling learning in the 21st century*. London: Facet.

Stiller, E. and LeBlanc, C. (2006) From Computer Literacy to Cyber-Literacy. *The Journal of Computer Sciences of Colleges*, 21(6): 4–13.

Swanson, T.A. (2004) A Radical Step: Implementing a Critical Information Literacy Model. *Libraries and the Academy*, 4: 259–73.

Thomas, S., Joseph, C., Laccetti, J., Mason, B., Mills, S., Perril, S. and Pullinger, K. (2007) *Transliteracy: Crossing Divides*. Available at *http://www.uic.edu/htbin/cgiwrap/bin/ojs/index.php/fm/article/viewArticle/2060/1908*.

Transliteracies Project. (2010) *Research in the Technological, Social, and Cultural Practices of Online Reading*. Available at *http://transliteracies.english.ucsb.edu/category/research-project*.

Tricarico, M.A., Von Daum Tholl, S. and O.Malley, E. (2001). Interactive Online Instruction for Library Research: The Small Academic Library Experience. *Journal of Academic Librarianship*, 27(3): 220.223.

Tyner, K. (1998) *Literacy in a Digital World: Teaching and Learning in the Age of Information*, Mahwah, NJ: Erlbaum Publishing.

Veldof, J. and Beavers, K. (2001). Going Mental: Tackling Mental Models for the Online Library Tutorial. *Research Strategies*, 18(1): 3–20.

Walsh, J. (2010). Controlling Disinformation on the Internet, Is MLI the answer? *Library Journal*, 59(7): 498–511.

Warnick, B. (2001) *Critical Literacy in a Digital Era: Technology, Rhetoric, and the Public Interest.* Mahwah, NJ: Lawrence Erlbaum Associates, Inc.

Wilder, S. (2005) Information Literacy Makes All the Wrong Assumptions. *Chronicle of Higher Education,* 51(18): B13.

Zhao, H., Plaisant, C. and Shneiderman, B. (2001) *Improving Accessibility and Usability of Geo-referenced Statistical Data.* Department of Computer Science & Human Computer Interaction Laboratory University of Maryland. Available at *http://hcil.cs.umd.edu/trs/2003-11/2003-11.html.*

# Appendix
# ACRL competencies, standards, performance indicators, and outcomes

## Standard One

The information literate student determines the nature and extent of the information needed. Performance Indicators:

1. The information literate student defines and articulates the need for information.

   *Outcomes include that they:*

   a. Confer with instructors and participates in class discussions, peer workgroups, and electronic discussions to identify a research topic, or other information need.

   b. Develop a thesis statement and formulate questions based on the information need.

   c. Explore general information sources to increase familiarity with the topic.

   d. Define or modify the information need to achieve a manageable focus.

   e. Identify key concepts and terms that describe the information need.

# Information Literacy Instruction

    f. Recognize that existing information can be combined with original thought, experimentation, and/or analysis to produce new information.

2. The information literate student identifies a variety of types and formats of potential sources for information.

   *Outcomes include that they:*

   a. Know how information is formally and informally produced, organized, and disseminated.

   b. Recognize that knowledge can be organized into disciplines that influence the way information is accessed.

   c. Identify the value and differences of potential resources in a variety of formats (e.g. multimedia, database, website, data set, audio/visual, book).

   d. Identify the purpose and audience of potential resources (e.g. popular vs. scholarly, current vs. historical).

   e. Differentiate between primary and secondary sources, recognizing how their use and importance vary with each discipline.

   f. Realize that information may need to be constructed with raw data from primary sources.

3. The information literate student considers the costs and benefits of acquiring the needed information.

   *Outcomes include that they:*

   a. Determine the availability of needed information and make decisions on broadening the information seeking process beyond local resources (e.g. interlibrary loan; using resources at other locations; obtaining images, videos, text, or sound).

b. Consider the feasibility of acquiring a new language or skill (e.g. foreign or discipline-based) in order to gather needed information and to understand its context.

c. Defines a realistic overall plan and timeline to acquire the needed information.

4. The information literate student reevaluates the nature and extent of the information need.

*Outcomes include that they:*

a. Review the initial information need to clarify, revise, or refine the question.

b. Describe criteria used to make information decisions and choices.

## Standard Two

The information literate student accesses needed information effectively and efficiently.

### *Performance Indicators:*

1. The information literate student selects the most appropriate investigative methods or information retrieval systems for accessing the needed information.

*Outcomes include that they:*

a. Identify appropriate investigative methods (e.g. laboratory experiment, simulation, fieldwork).

b. Investigate benefits and applicability of various investigative methods.

c. Investigate the scope, content, and organization of information retrieval systems.

d. Select efficient and effective approaches for accessing the information needed from the investigative method or information retrieval system.

2. The information literate student constructs and implements effectively-designed search strategies.

*Outcomes include that they:*

a. Develop a research plan appropriate to the investigative method.

b. Identify keywords, synonyms and related terms for the information needed.

c. Select controlled vocabulary specific to the discipline or information retrieval source.

d. Construct a search strategy using appropriate commands for the information retrieval system selected (e.g. Boolean operators, truncation, and proximity for search engines; internal organizers such as indexes for books).

e. Implement the search strategy in various information retrieval systems using different user interfaces and search engines, with different command languages, protocols, and search parameters.

f. Implement the search using investigative protocols appropriate to the discipline.

3. The information literate student retrieves information online or in person using a variety of methods.

*Outcomes include that they:*

a. Use various search systems to retrieve information in a variety of formats.

b. Use various classification schemes and other systems (e.g. call number systems or indexes) to locate information resources within the library or to identify specific sites for physical exploration.

c. Use specialized online or in-person services available at the institution to retrieve information needed (e.g. interlibrary loan/document delivery, professional associations, institutional research offices, community resources, experts and practitioners).

d. Use surveys, letters, interviews, and other forms of inquiry to retrieve primary information.

4. The information literate student refines the search strategy if necessary.

*Outcomes include that they:*

a. Assess the quantity, quality, and relevance of the search results to determine whether alternative information retrieval systems or investigative methods should be utilized.

b. Identify gaps in the information retrieved and determine if the search strategy should be revised.

c. Repeat the search using the revised strategy as necessary.

5. The information literate student extracts, records, and manages the information and its sources.

*Outcomes include that they:*

a. Select among various technologies the most appropriate one for the task of extracting the needed information (e.g. copy/paste software functions, photocopier, scanner, audio/visual equipment, or exploratory instruments).

b. Create a system for organizing the information.

c. Differentiate between the types of sources cited and understands the elements and correct syntax of a citation for a wide range of resources.

d. Record all pertinent citation information for future reference.

e. Use various technologies to manage the information selected and organized.

## Standard Three

The information literate student evaluates information and its sources critically and incorporates selected information into his or her knowledge base and value system.

## *Performance Indicators:*

1. The information literate student summarizes the main ideas to be extracted from the information gathered.

   *Outcomes include that they:*

   a. Read the text and select main ideas.

   b. Restate textual concepts in their own words and select data accurately.

   c. Identify verbatim material that can be then appropriately quoted.

2. The information literate student articulates and applies initial criteria for evaluating both the information and its sources.

   *Outcomes include that they:*

   a. Examine and compare information from various sources in order to evaluate reliability, validity, accuracy, authority, timeliness, and point of view or bias.

b. Analyze the structure and logic of supporting arguments or methods.

   c. Recognize prejudice, deception, or manipulation.

   d. Recognize the cultural, physical, or other context within which the information was created and understands the impact of context on interpreting the information.

3. The information literate student synthesizes main ideas to construct new concepts.

   *Outcomes include that they:*

   a. Recognize interrelationships among concepts and combines them into potentially useful primary statements with supporting evidence.

   b. Extend initial synthesis, when possible, at a higher level of abstraction to construct new hypotheses that may require additional information.

   c. Utilize computer and other technologies (e.g. spreadsheets, databases, multimedia, and audio or visual equipment) for studying the interaction of ideas and other phenomena.

4. The information literate student compares new knowledge with prior knowledge to determine the value added, contradictions, or other unique characteristics of the information.

   *Outcomes include that they:*

   a. Determine whether information satisfies the research or other information need.

   b. Use consciously selected criteria to determine whether the information contradicts or verifies information used from other sources.

   c. Draw conclusions based upon information gathered.

d. Test theories with discipline-appropriate techniques (e.g. simulators, experiments).
   e. Determine probable accuracy by questioning the source of the data, the limitations of the information gathering tools or strategies, and the reasonableness of the conclusions.
   f. Integrate new information with previous information or knowledge.
   g. Select information that provides evidence for the topic.
5. The information literate student determines whether the new knowledge has an impact on the individual's value system and takes steps to reconcile differences.

   *Outcomes include that they:*
   a. Investigate differing viewpoints encountered in the literature.
   b. Determine whether to incorporate or reject viewpoints encountered.
6. The information literate student validates understanding and interpretation of the information through discourse with other individuals, subject-area experts, and/or practitioners.

   *Outcomes include that they:*
   a. Participate in classroom and other discussions.
   b. Participate in class-sponsored electronic communication forums designed to encourage discourse on the topic (e.g. e-mail, bulletin boards, chat rooms).
   c. Seek expert opinion through a variety of mechanisms (e.g. interviews, e-mail, listservs).
7. The information literate student determines whether the initial query should be revised.

*Outcomes include that they:*

a. Determine if original information need has been satisfied or if additional information is needed.

b. Review search strategy and incorporates additional concepts as necessary.

c. Review information retrieval sources used and expands to include others as needed.

## Standard Four

The information literate student, individually or as a member of a group, uses information effectively to accomplish a specific purpose.

### *Performance Indicators:*

1. The information literate student applies new and prior information to the planning and creation of a particular product or performance.

   *Outcomes include that they:*

   a. Organize the content in a manner that supports the purposes and format of the product or performance (e.g. outlines, drafts, storyboards).

   b. Articulate knowledge and skills transferred from prior experiences to planning and creating the product or performance.

   c. Integrate the new and prior information, including quotations and paraphrasings, in a manner that supports the purposes of the product or performance.

d. Manipulate digital text, images, and data, as needed, transferring them from their original locations and formats to a new context.

2. The information literate student revises the development process for the product or performance.

    *Outcomes include that they:*

    a. Maintain a journal or log of activities related to the information seeking, evaluating, and communicating process.

    b. Reflect on past successes, failures, and alternative strategies.

3. The information literate student communicates the product or performance effectively to others.

    *Outcomes include that they:*

    a. Choose a communication medium and format that best supports the purposes of the product or performance and the intended audience.

    b. Use a range of information technology applications in creating the product or performance.

    c. Incorporate principles of design and communication.

    d. Communicate clearly and with a style that supports the purposes of the intended audience.

## Standard Five

The information literate student understands many of the economic, legal, and social issues surrounding the use of information and accesses and uses information ethically and legally.

Appendix

## *Performance Indicators:*

1. The information literate student understands many of the ethical, legal and socio-economic issues surrounding information and information technology.

   *Outcomes include that they:*

   a. Identify and discuss issues related to privacy and security in both the print and electronic environments.

   b. Identify and discuss issues related to free vs. fee-based access to information.

   c. Identify and discuss issues related to censorship and freedom of speech.

   d. Demonstrate an understanding of intellectual property, copyright, and fair use of copyrighted material.

2. The information literate student follows laws, regulations, institutional policies, and etiquette related to the access and use of information resources.

   *Outcomes include that they:*

   a. Participate in electronic discussions following accepted practices (e.g. 'Netiquette').

   b. Use approved passwords and other forms of ID for access to information resources.

   c. Comply with institutional policies on access to information resources.

   d. Preserve the integrity of information resources, equipment, systems and facilities.

   e. Legally obtain, store, and disseminate text, data, images, or sounds.

# Information Literacy Instruction

    f. Demonstrate an understanding of what constitutes plagiarism and does not represent work attributable to others as their own.

    g. Demonstrate an understanding of institutional policies related to human subjects research.

3. The information literate student acknowledges the use of information sources in communicating the product or performance.

*Outcomes include that they:*

    a. Select an appropriate documentation style and use it consistently to cite sources.

    b. Post permission granted notices, as needed, for copyrighted material.

# Index

academic libraries, 114–16
ACRL Competencies, 70–1, 76, 77, 84–5, 185–96
   Standard Five, 194–6
   Standard Four, 193–4
   Standard One, 185–7
   Standard Three, 190–3
   Standard Two, 187–90
ACRL *Standards*, 79
active learning, 23–4, 135
   vs traditional learning, 138–40
active learning instruction, 21–36
   active learning, 23–4
   cooperative learning, 24–8
   collaborative learning, 28–32
      jigsaw method and exercise, 30–2
      vs traditional library classroom, 29
   curriculum, 25–7
   problem-based learning, 32–6
      lesson development questions and learning outcomes, 35
active participation, 138
affective changes, 135–7
affective outcomes
   measuring ILI effectiveness, 86–95
American Association of School Libraries (AASL), 4
Americans with Disabilities Act (ADA), 110
andragogy, 103
Ardis, S., 7–8
Aronson, E., 30
Association of College and Research Libraries (ACRL), 4, 58
asynchronous instruction, 7

Bandura, A., 88
behavioral changes, 130–2
behavioral outcomes
   measuring ILI effectiveness, 60–9
Beile, J., 90
Blackboard, 122
Bloom taxonomy, 71
Boote, D., 90
Bostick, S., 92
Breivik, P., 6–7
Bruce, C., 4

Cahoy, E., 86–7
censorship, 157
Center for Social Marketing and Behavioral Change, 130
cognitive changes, 132–5
cognitive outcomes
   measuring ILI effectiveness, 70–86

Colvin, J., 75
Colvin-Kleene (CK) Model, 75, 77
computer assisted instruction, 36–41
  modules, 38–9
  vs traditional lecture, 140–1
course-integrated sessions, 120
critical literacy, 166
cyber literacy, 165–6
  competencies, 167

Dewey, M., 5–6
disinformation, 154–5
D2L, 122
Doyle, C., 4
drill-and-practice systems, 121–2
drive-by bibliographic instruction, 121
drop-in instruction, 121

electronic instruction, 121–3
Elluminate Live video conferencing software, 122
epistemology, 155

face-to-face (FTF) learning groups, 118–21
face-to-face instruction, 130, 133, 136, 144
foundationalism, 162, 165
fully automated reference instruction, 174–5

Gilchrist, D., 34
Google PageRank, 169
Google PageRank Checker, 169
Gurian, M., 107

Hotchkiss, P., 60

inaccurate information, 154
independent learning, 142–3
information literacy, 3–8, 158
  and cognitive skills, 76
  process, 78
*Information Literacy Competency Standards for Higher Education*, 70–1, 79, 86
information literacy instruction, 3–8, 163–4
  curriculum
    ENG 101 class, 12–13
    PSY 101 class, 13–15
  definition, 3–5
  development, 5–8
  fully automated reference instruction, 174–5
  future trends, 153–76
  marketing/information literacy comparison, 8
  measuring ACRL competency standards, 84–5
  measuring effectiveness, 59–95
    affective outcomes, 86–95
    behavioral outcomes, 60–9
    cognitive outcomes, 70–86
    cross-impact grid, 75
    information literacy and cognitive skills, 76
    information literacy process, 78
    levels of cognitive learning, 74
    Library Anxiety Scale, 94
    library usage questionnaire, 62
    list of standardized knowledge tests, 80–3

# Index

pretest/posttest research design, 68
questionnaire on information seeking behavior, 63–7
revised Bloom taxonomy, 72–4
terms associated with the concept of affect by various authors, 87
methods of instruction, 3–51
   active learning instruction, 21–36
   computer assisted instruction, 36–41
   evaluation form for websites, 15–17
   learner-centered instruction, 41–5
   list of teaching methods, 10
   self-directed, independent learning, 45–50
   teaching methods, 9–50
   traditional instruction, 9–21
multi-literacy instruction, 154–72
objectives of instruction, 57–96
participant populations, library environments and learning environments, 101–25
   learning environments, 117–23
   learning objectives of adult learners' workshops, 105–6
   library environments, 112–17
   participants, 102–12
role of assessment, 57–9
social psychology, 175–6
transliteracies, 172–3

information literacy instruction (ILI) methods, 127–48
   choosing based on learning environment comparison, 143–6
   choosing based on objective, 129–38
   choosing based on teaching method comparison, 138–43
   factors, 128–9
information officer, 117
information scientist, 117
information seeking behavior, 61–2, 69
   questionnaire, 63–7
inlinks, 169
Internet, 155
   information evaluation criteria, 160–1

jigsaw activity, 43
'Jigsaw Method,' 30–2
just-in-time sessions, 120–1

Keene, J., 72
Kenney, B., 8
Knapp, P., 6
knowledge, 155
Knowles, M., 103
Krikelas, J., 62
Kuhlthau, C., 4
Kurbanoglu, S., 88–9

learner-centered instruction, 41–5
   jigsaw activity, 44
   vs teacher-centered instruction, 42
   vs traditional lecture, 141–2
learning environment, 117–23, 143–6

electronic instruction, 121–3
face-to-face learning groups, 118–21
librarians, 4
library anxiety, 91–5, 136–7
Library Anxiety Scale (LAS), 60, 92–5
library environments, 112–17
  academic libraries, 114–16
  public libraries, 113–14
  special libraries, 116–17
library instruction, 6–7
library participants, 5, 102–12
  types of participants, 102–12
    abilities, 111–12
    age, 102–7
    ethnicity and multiculturalism, 108–11
    gender, 107–8
*Library Trends*, 61
library usage, 60, 61, 68
Lorenzen, M., 43

Mellon, C., 92
Microsoft, 175
misinformation, 154
Moodle, 122
Mueller, J., 79
multi-literacy instruction, 154–72
  accuracy evaluation criteria, 168–9
  competencies, 167
  Internet information evaluation criteria, 160–1
  learning objectives, 164
multi literacy, 170

nature-based teaching, 108
non-traditional student, 102–7

one-shot library instruction, 120–1
'one-shots,' 7
online tutorial, 144–6

program objective, 129–38
  affective changes, 135–7
  behavioral changes, 130–2
  cognitive changes, 132–5
  method selection, 138
public libraries, 113–14

quality certification, 157

re-entry learners, 103
Ren, W-H., 89

Samson, S., 79
Schroeder, R., 86–7
screencasting software, 122
self-directed independent learning, 45–50
  library skills worksheet, 46–8
  vs traditional learning, 142–3
self-efficacy, 88–91, 136–7
simulation, 121–2
social psychology, 175–6
Socratic Method, 22
special libraries, 116–17
stand-alone courses, 120
Stover, M., 39
streaming media, 17–21
Switzer, A., 108–9
synchronous instruction, 7

teacher-centered instruction, 42
teaching method, 138–43
  traditional lecture vs active learning, 138–40

traditional lecture vs computer-assisted instruction, 140–1
traditional lecture vs learner-centered instruction, 141–2
traditional lecture vs self-directed independent learning, 142–3
traditional instruction (TI), 9–21
traditional lecture
 vs active learning, 138–40
 vs computer-assisted instruction, 140–1
 vs learner-centered instruction, 141–2
 vs self-directed independent learning, 142–3
transliteracies, 172–3

video conferencing software, 122
video instruction, 18–21

web-based tutorial (WBT), 36

CPSIA information can be obtained at www.ICGtesting.com
Printed in the USA
BVOW040006051011

272831BV00002B/7/P

9 781843 346272